Number Tools

Number

HOLT, RINEHART AND WINSTON

Mathematics in Context is a comprehensive curriculum for the middle grades. It was developed in 1991 through 1997 in collaboration with the Wisconsin Center for Education Research, School of Education, University of Wisconsin-Madison and the Freudenthal Institute at the University of Utrecht, The Netherlands, with the support of the National Science Foundation Grant No. 9054928.

This unit is a new unit prepared as a part of the revision of the curriculum carried out in 2003 through 2005, with the support of the National Science Foundation Grant No. ESI 0137414.

Kindt, M, Dekker, T., Burrill, G., and Romberg T. A. (2006). *Number tools.* In Wisconsin Center for Education Research & Freudenthal Institute (Eds.), Mathematics in Context. Chicago: Encyclopædia Britannica, Inc.

ISBN 0-03-040384-7

1 2 3 4 5 6 073 09 08 07 06 05

The *Mathematics in Context* Development Team

Development 1991–1997

The initial version of *Number Tools* was developed by Frans Van Galen and Marja van den Heuvel-Panhuizen. It was adapted for use in American Schools by Margaret A. Pligge.

Wisconsin Center for Education Research Staff

Thomas A. Romberg
Director

Joan Daniels Pedro
Assistant to the Director

Gail Burrill
Coordinator

Margaret R. Meyer
Coordinator

Project Staff

Jonathan Brendefur
Laura Brinker
James Browne
Jack Burrill
Rose Byrd
Peter Christiansen
Barbara Clarke
Doug Clarke
Beth R. Cole
Fae Dremock
Mary Ann Fix

Sherian Foster
James A, Middleton
Jasmina Milinkovic
Margaret A. Pligge
Mary C. Shafer
Julia A. Shew
Aaron N. Simon
Marvin Smith
Stephanie Z. Smith
Mary S. Spence

Freudenthal Institute Staff

Jan de Lange
Director

Els Feijs
Coordinator

Martin van Reeuwijk
Coordinator

Mieke Abels
Nina Boswinkel
Frans van Galen
Koeno Gravemeijer
Marja van den Heuvel-Panhuizen
Jan Auke de Jong
Vincent Jonker
Ronald Keijzer
Martin Kindt

Jansie Niehaus
Nanda Querelle
Anton Roodhardt
Leen Streefland
Adri Treffers
Monica Wijers
Astrid de Wild

Revision 2003–2005

The revised version of *Number Tools* was developed by Mieke Abels, Truus Dekker, and Nanda Querelle and was adapted for use in American Schools by Margaret A. Pligge and Margaret R. Meyer.

Wisconsin Center for Education Research Staff

Thomas A. Romberg
Director

David C. Webb
Coordinator

Gail Burrill
Editorial Coordinator

Margaret A. Pligge
Editorial Coordinator

Project Staff

Sarah Ailts
Beth R. Cole
Erin Hazlett
Teri Hedges
Karen Hoiberg
Carrie Johnson
Jean Krusi
Elaine McGrath

Margaret R. Meyer
Anne Park
Bryna Rappaport
Kathleen A. Steele
Ana C. Stephens
Candace Ulmer
Jill Vettrus

Freudenthal Institute Staff

Jan de Lange
Director

Truus Dekker
Coordinator

Mieke Abels
Content Coordinator

Monica Wijers
Content Coordinator

Arthur Bakker
Peter Boon
Els Feijs
Dédé de Haan
Martin Kindt

Nathalie Kuijpers
Huub Nilwik
Sonia Palha
Nanda Querelle
Martin van Reeuwijk

Cover photo credits: (left to right) © Getty Images; © Comstock Images; © Digital Vision

Illustrations
7–11, 14 (top), **22, 35, 36, 66, 70, 74, 77, 79, 82, 85–87** (top), **94, 126, 127,** Christine McCabe/© Encyclopædia Britannica, Inc.

Photographs
99 Minnesota Museum of the Mississippi

Contents

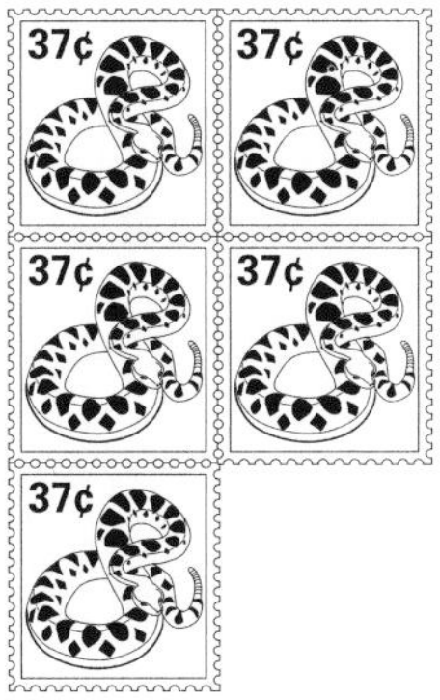

37¢
37¢
37¢
37¢
37¢

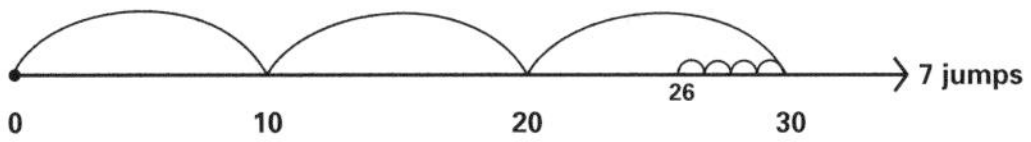

0
10
20
26
30
7 jumps

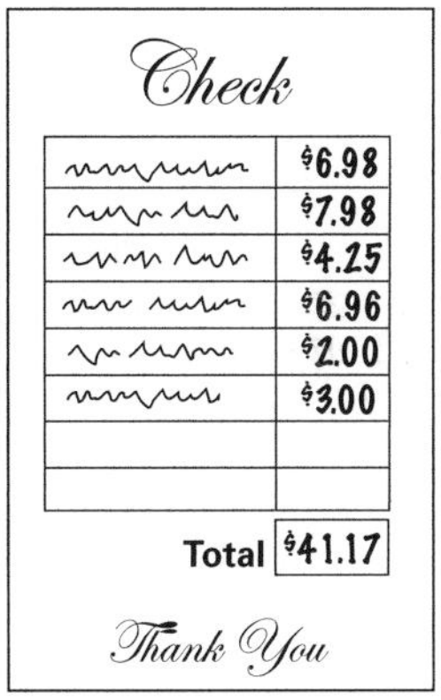

Check
$6.98
$7.98
$4.25
$6.96
$2.00
$3.00
Total $41.17
Thank You

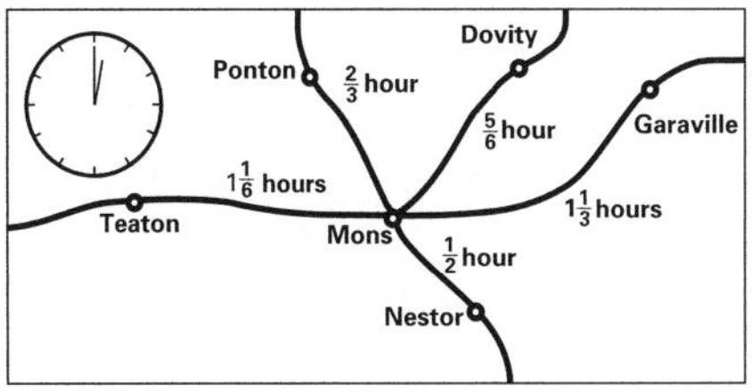

Dovity
Ponton
$\frac{2}{3}$ hour
$\frac{5}{6}$ hour
Garaville
$1\frac{1}{6}$ hours
Teaton
$1\frac{1}{3}$ hours
Mons
$\frac{1}{2}$ hour
Nestor

Contents

small box envelope certificate
large box

50 cm
60 cm
40 cm

24 students

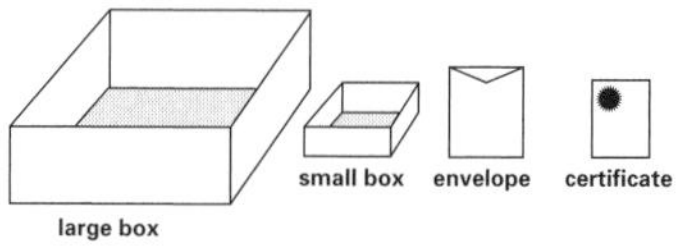

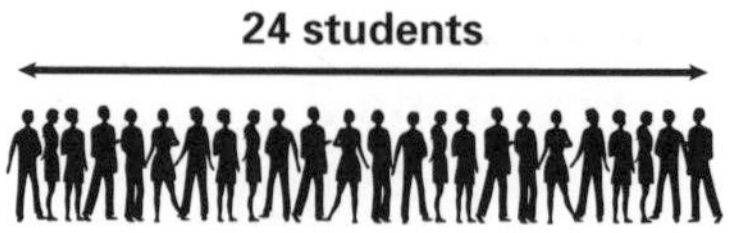

Contents

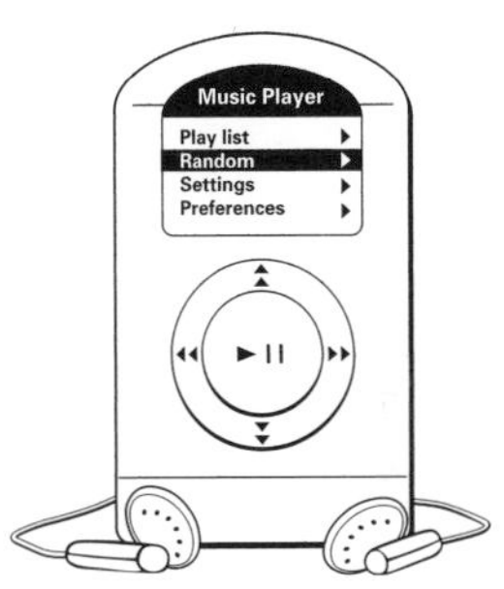

thousands
hundreds
tens
ones
2
3
5
1
Music Player
Play list
Random
Settings
Preferences

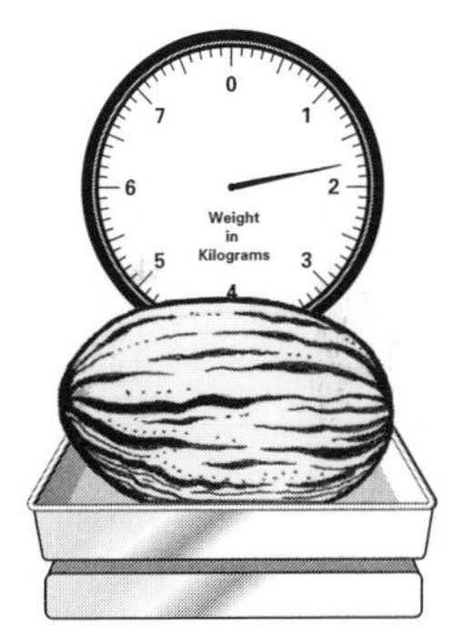

Weight in Kilograms

Name ______________________ Date ____________ Class ____________

What's in a Number?

How would you describe the number 52? You might say:

52 is 2 × 26;

52 is 4 × 13;

52 is two quarters and two pennies; or

52 is the age of Anton's father.

1. Write down several other ways to describe the number 52.

2. Write down several ways to describe the number 12.

3. Write down several ways to describe the number 24.

4. Choose your favorite number, and describe it in several ways.

Name ______________________ Date __________ Class __________

The Plus or Minus Operations Game

The Plus or Minus Operations Game

Number of players: Two or more

Rules:

- Each player must reach a target number by adding and/or subtracting a list of numbers.
- Players must use all of the numbers at least once.
- Players may use some numbers more than once.
- The winner is the player who reaches the target number using the fewest operations.

Example:

Judy used 5 operations: 3 + 5 + 9 + 10 + 3 − 5 = 25.

Maritza used 6 operations: 3 + 5 + 9 + 10 + 10 − 9 − 3 = 25.

Judy won, because she used only five operations while Maritza used six.

Play the game with the following numbers:

1. 3 6 7 8 → 39

2. 3 5 4 9 → 32

3. 17 20 8 10 → 74

4. 5 11 16 4 → 53

5. 15 8 14 20 → 91

6. 13 9 15 12 → 68

7. Make up two of your own problems.

Name ______________________ Date ____________ Class ____________

Alphonse and Sarah decided to do their homework together. They soon discovered their worksheet had gotten wet, and the ink had blotted some of the numbers. One problem on the worksheet looked like this:

6 x 4 =

1. How many different answers could this problem have?

At first, they thought they could not do the problem. Alphonse decided to be creative and wrote this answer, "The product is more than 240 and less than 294." Sarah agreed but thought that the answer could also include the numbers 240 and 294.

2. Who is correct? Explain why you agree with Sarah or Alphonse.

Ms. Marne complimented Alphonse and Sarah for being diligent in completing their work! The class discussion was thought provoking, so she decided to make up some more blot-problems.

3. Find the range of possible answers to these blot problems. For each problem, the blot covers only one digit.

	The answer ranges from...		The answer ranges from...
a. **8 × 3 =**	______ to ______	f. **6 × 5 =**	______ to ______
b. **5 × 7 =**	______ to ______	g. **5 × 2 =**	______ to ______
c. **7 × 8 =**	______ to ______	h. **3 × 3 =**	______ to ______
d. **4 × 2 =**	______ to ______	i. **6 × 4 =**	______ to ______
e. **3 × 9 =**	______ to ______	j. **9 × 3 =**	______ to ______

Name ______________________ Date __________ Class __________

Blots (page 2)

4. Find the range of possible answers to these blot-problems. In each problem, the second number is a three-digit number.

	The answer ranges from...
a. **3 × 3■■ =**	______ to ______
b. **6 × 4■2 =**	______ to ______
c. **9 × 2■0 =**	______ to ______
d. **4 × 6■9 =**	______ to ______
e. **8 × 53■ =**	______ to ______
f. **2 × 25■ =**	______ to ______
g. **3 × 62■ =**	______ to ______
h. **6 × 54■ =**	______ to ______
i. **3 × ■70 =**	______ to ______
j. **7 × 24■ =**	______ to ______

5. Which problems were easiest? Which were more challenging?

Name ______________________ Date ____________ Class ____________

Raffle Tickets (page 1)

This year, Johnson School is celebrating its 80th anniversary by having a Jubilee with live music and a raffle. Local businesses have donated items for the raffle. During the celebration, students will sell raffle tickets to raise money for the school library.

Here is a packet of raffle tickets that Sandra plans to sell. Notice that each raffle ticket has a number and the tickets are in numerical order.

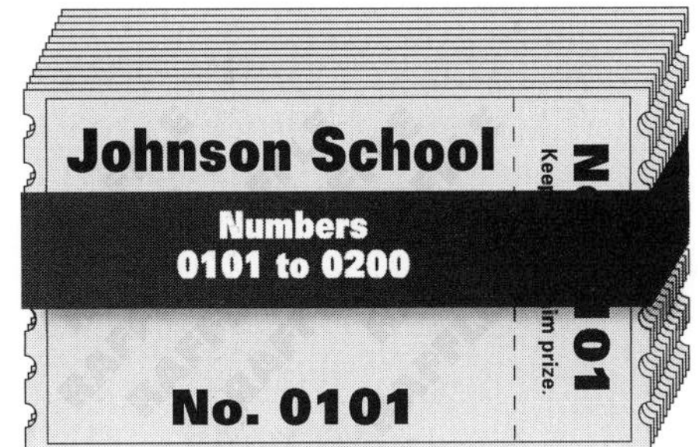

1. List a few of Sandra's ticket numbers.

Gill's packet of raffle tickets number from 0401 to 0500.

2. List a few of Gill's ticket numbers.

Mary's packet of raffle tickets number from 1201 to 1300.

3. List a few of Mary's ticket numbers.

4. Do Sandra, Gill, and Mary have the same number of tickets to sell? Explain.

Here is Chantrea's packet of raffle tickets after selling some tickets. The number of the ticket on the top of her packet is No. 3414.

5. What ticket numbers were in Chantrea's original packet? How do you know?

6. How many tickets has Chantrea sold so far?

Name ______________________ Date ______________ Class ______________

Raffle Tickets (page 2)

Mr. Han is one of the parents attending the party at the Jubilee. He buys several tickets.

7. If his first ticket is No.1235 and his last ticket is No. 1247, how many tickets did Mr. Han buy?
8. From which student did Mr. Han buy his tickets? How do you know?

At the end of the celebration, students must turn in their leftover tickets along with the money they collected. Here is the packet Sandra turned in. She sold up to ticket No. 0178.

9. How many tickets did Sandra turn in?

Here are Gill and Mary's leftover tickets.

Gill's Tickets

Mary's Tickets

10. How many tickets did each person turn in?

Franklin, Marilyn, and Camilla go to the post office to buy some stamps.

The postal worker shows them a part of a sheet and says, "This is all I have of this stamp. Is this enough?" How many stamps did she show them? Here is their discussion on how to calculate the number of stamps on the sheet.

Franklin:

I would calculate 4 times 10 and then add 3.

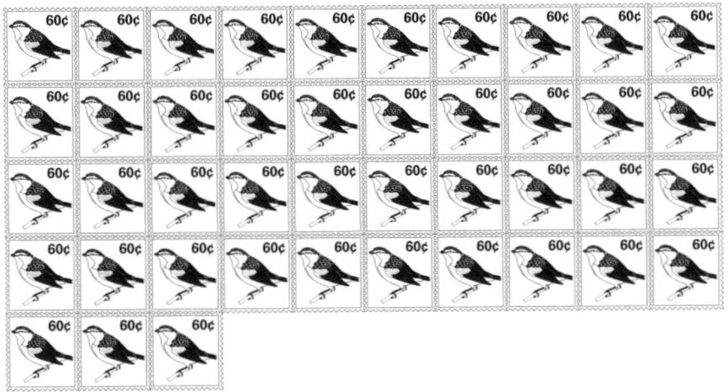

Marilyn:

I would calculate 3 times 5, and then 7 times 4, and then add the two answers.

Camilla:

I would calculate 5 times 10, and then subtract 7.

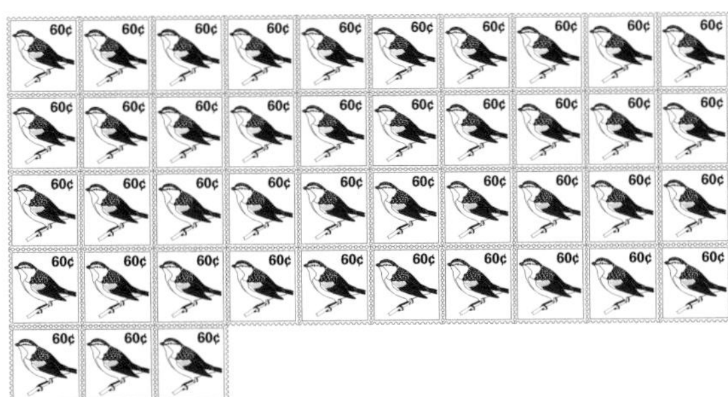

1. Use the pictures of the stamps to explain each strategy.

You can summarize each strategy by writing an expression using parentheses and operation signs. For example, the expression summarizing Franklin's strategy is $(4 \times 10) + 3$.

2. Summarize each of the other two strategies by writing an expression using parentheses and operation signs.

Name ______________________ Date ____________ Class ____________

Working at the Post Office (page 2)

3. Write how you would find the total number of stamps in each set. Summarize your strategy by writing an expression using parentheses and operation signs.

a.

b.

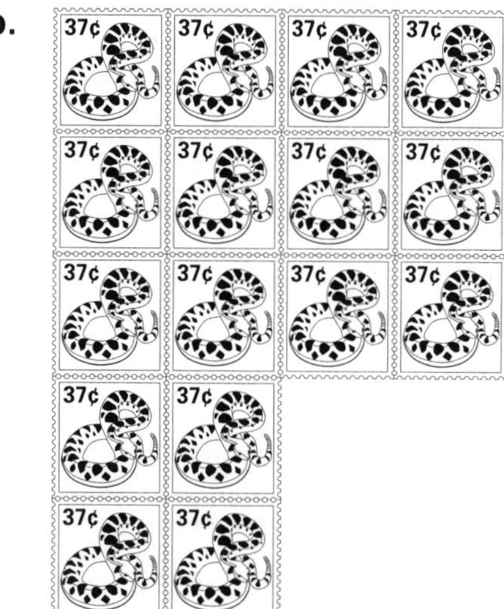

c.

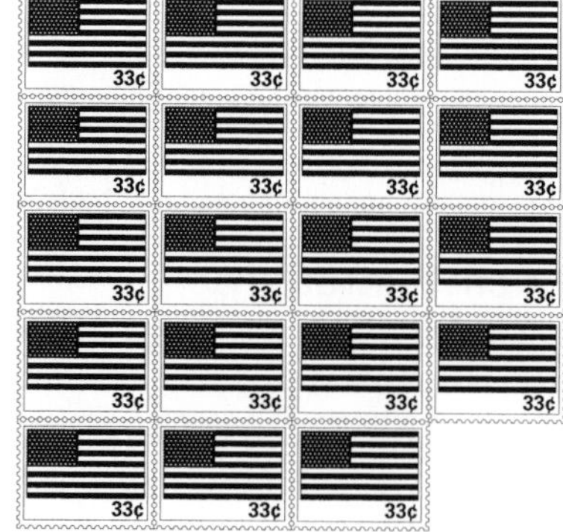

4. Find a new strategy to calculate the stamp sets in problem 3. Write a different expression to describe your new strategy.

Name ________________________ Date ______________ Class ______________

1. When Mr. Lee buys stamps, he pays with bills and never carries coins or plastic. Estimate how much money Mr. Lee will give the postal worker to purchase each of the following sets of stamps.

a.

c.

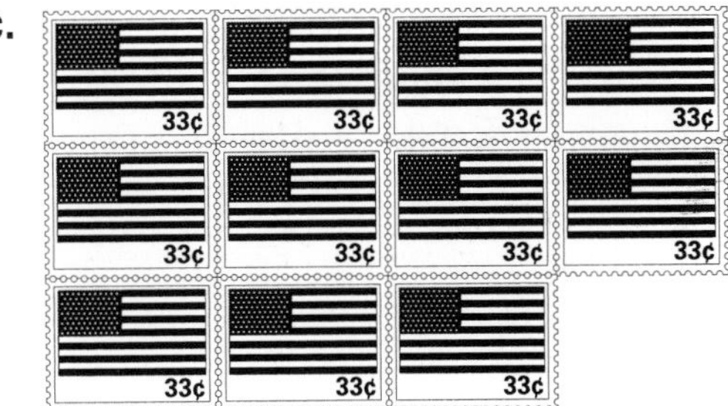

b.

d.

Name ______________________ Date ____________ Class ____________

Costs (page 2)

2. Here are sets of stamps that people can buy at the post office. Calculate the cost without the use of a calculator.

a. 37¢ stamps, featuring American Indian artifacts, available in a sheet of 10.
Cost:

b. Lewis and Clark
37¢ stamps in a book of 20.
Cost:

c. Cloudscapes
37¢ stamps, in a sheet of 15.
Cost:

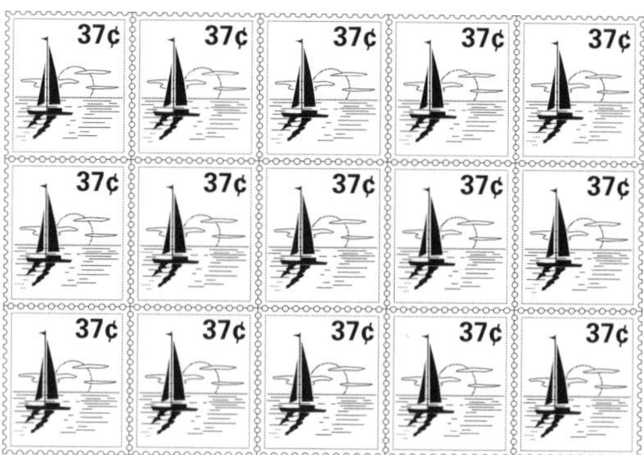

d. How can you use the answer for problem **a** to find the cost in **b**?

e. How can you use the answer for problem **a** to find the cost in **c**?

Name ______________________ Date__________ Class__________

3. For each of the following sets, calculate the cost without using a calculator or pencil and paper. Then show how you mentally calculated the answer.

a. 

Wilma Rudolph
23¢ stamps, in a book of 10
Cost:
Mental steps:

b. 

George Washington
23¢ stamps, in a book of 20
Cost:
Mental steps:

c. 

Love Special
60¢ stamps, in a sheet of 20
Cost:
Mental steps:

d. 

Antique Toys
37¢ stamps, in a roll of 100
Cost:
Mental steps:

e. 

Greetings From America
Sheet of 50 Self-Adhesive 37¢
Cost:
Mental steps:

f. 

American Indian Artifacts
37¢ stamps in a pack of
5 books of 20 stamps
Cost:
Mental steps:

Name ________________________ Date __________ Class __________

The Goal Game

Simone secretly entered exactly five keystrokes on her calculator. She writes down the buttons she pressed, but not the order she pressed them.

After she presses the = button, she shows everyone her calculator display. It shows the number 636.

1. What is the order Simone pressed the buttons? There is only one possibility that produces an answer of 636.

You have just played the Goal Game. Simone was the goalkeeper. She wrote down the five buttons she used and showed the answer on her calculator display. The answer displayed is the Goal Number. You had to figure out the order she used. If you match the Goal Number within two minutes, you score a goal for one point.

2. Play the Goal Game in pairs or small groups.

Game rules

- Use any five of these calculator buttons:

To prepare:

The goalkeeper secretly uses his or her calculator to record the 5 buttons and make the Goal Number answer appear in the calculator displays. (The goalkeeper might also make a secret record of the order of the keystrokes.)

To play:

The goalkeeper writes the five buttons and shows the Goal Number to the players. The goalkeeper begins timing for two minutes.

At the end of two minutes, players show their calculator display. If a player matches the Goal Number, that player must recreate the order of the keystrokes for the group. Players recreating the Goal Number score a goal and earn one point. Each player takes a turn being the goalkeeper.

The winner:

The winner is the player who earns the most points after everyone has a turn being the goalkeeper.

Name ______________________ Date__________ Class__________

Shoveling Sidewalks

On days when it snows, Raúl and his friends shovel their neighbors' sidewalks. For each different day below, color the part of the sidewalks each person shovels. Assume the people shovel equal amounts and that the group shovels all the sidewalks shown. Use fractions to describe the part of a sidewalk each helper shovels.

Day | **Sidewalks** | **Raúl and his friends**

1. Each helper shovels:

2. Each helper shovels:

3. Each helper shovels:

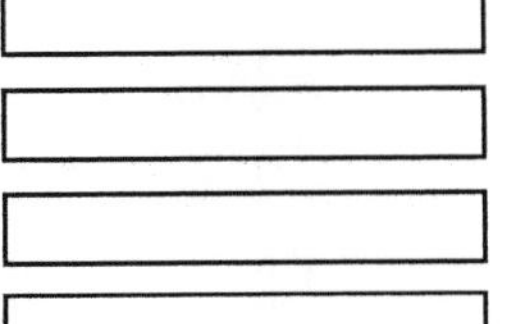

4. Each helper shovels:

Name ______________________ Date ____________ Class ____________

Modeling Clay

Mike, Liz, and Jordan want to share this bar of modeling clay.

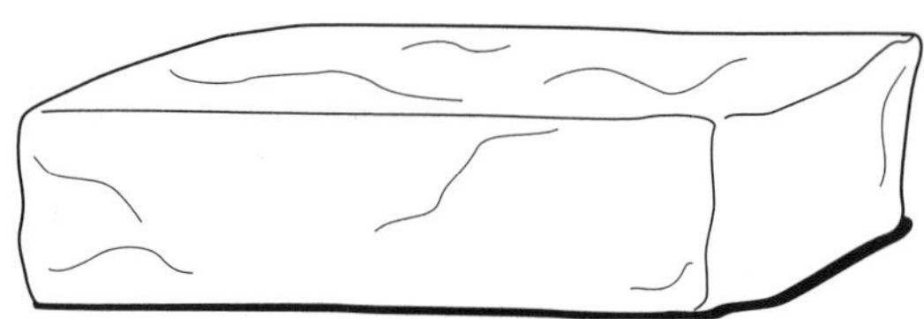

1. Make a drawing of the bar and shade one person's share. Write one person's share as a fraction of the bar.

2. For each example below, write a fraction to represent the part of the bar that is shaded.

a. 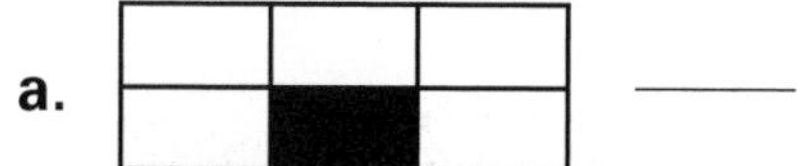 ______

b.  ______

c.  ______

d. 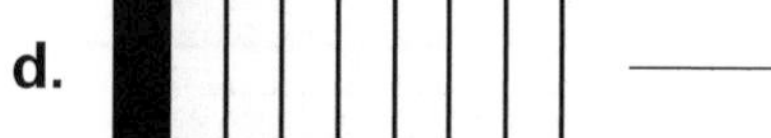 ______

e. 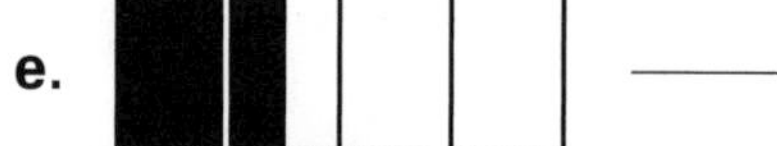 ______

f. ______

g.  ______

h. ______

i. ______

j. ______

k. ______

l. ______

m. ______

n. ______

o. ______

p. ______

q. ______

r. ______

s. ______

t. ______

Name ______________________ Date ______________ Class ______________

Measuring Cups

Use an arrow to indicate the level of each measuring cup after the ingredients have been added.

Here you see an example showing that the level of the liquid is $\frac{1}{2}$ cup.

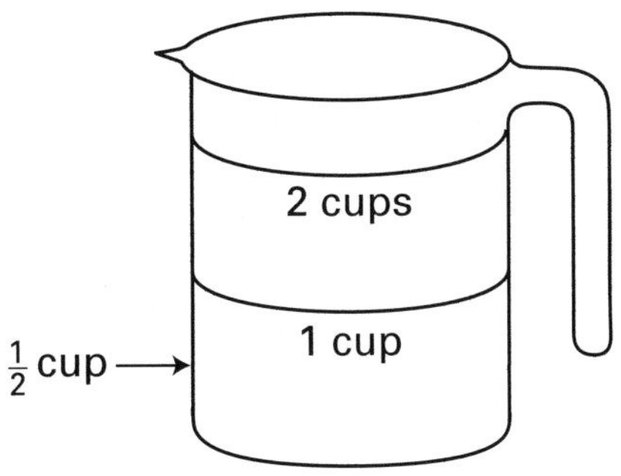

1.

2 cups
1 cup

$\frac{1}{4}$ cup

2.

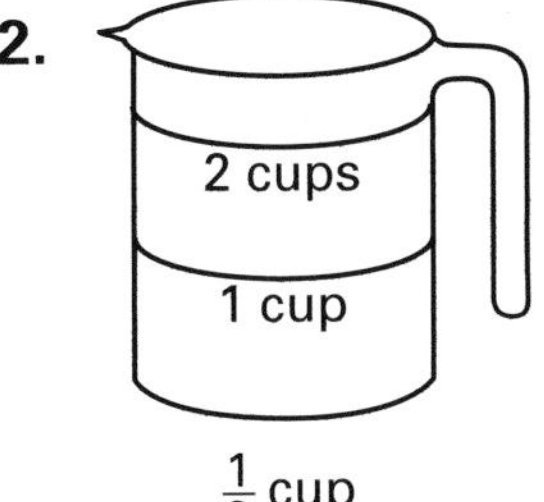

$\frac{1}{3}$ cup

3.

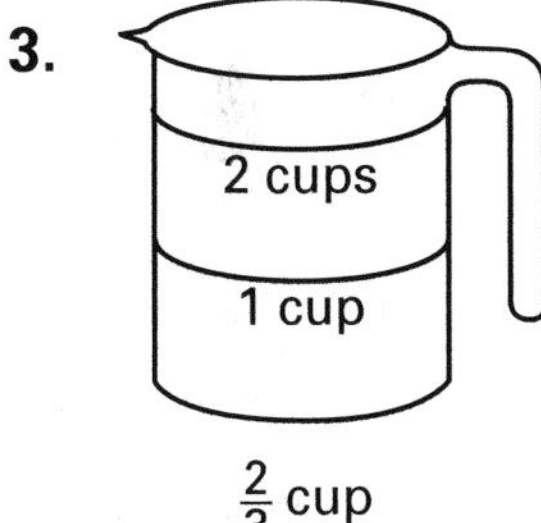

$\frac{2}{3}$ cup

4.

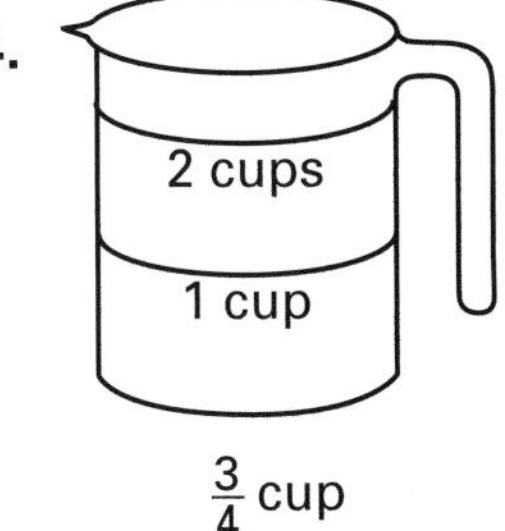

$\frac{3}{4}$ cup

5.

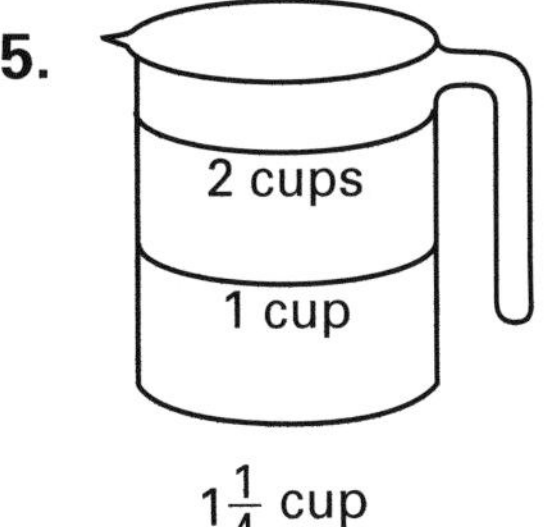

$1\frac{1}{4}$ cup

6.

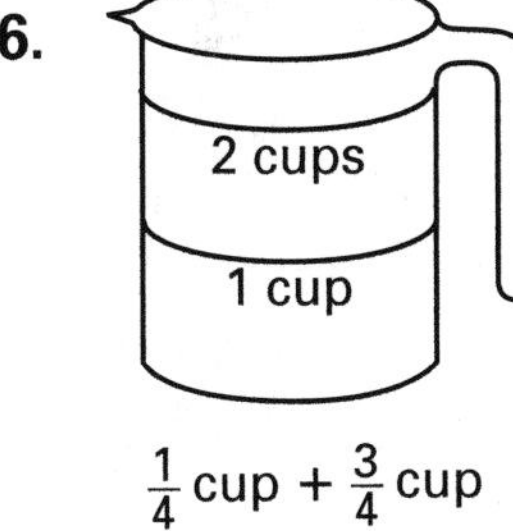

$\frac{1}{4}$ cup + $\frac{3}{4}$ cup

7.

$\frac{2}{3}$ cup + $\frac{2}{3}$ cup

8.

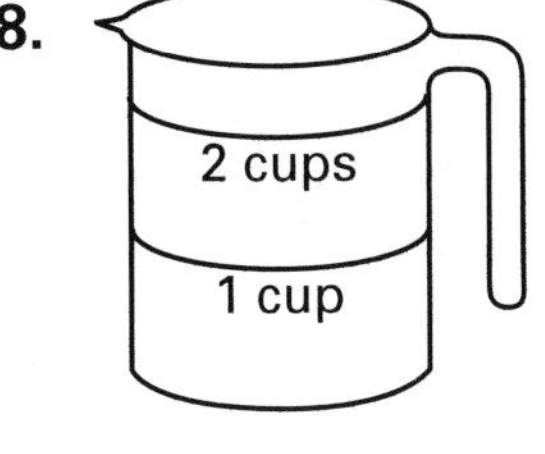

$\frac{3}{4}$ cup + $\frac{1}{2}$ cup

9.

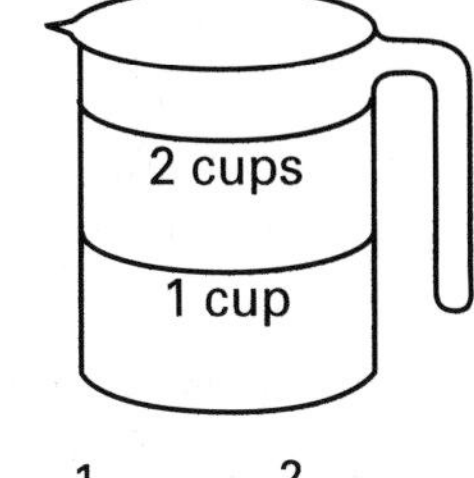

$\frac{1}{2}$ cup + $\frac{2}{3}$ cup

Name ______________ Date __________ Class __________

The Jump, Jump Game (page 1 of 2)

Object of the Game:

Use a number line to "jump" from one number to another in as *few jumps as possible*. Compare your score with a partner.

To Play:

To get to a number, you can make *jumps of only three lengths: 1, 10, and 100.* You can show your jumps on the number line by drawing curves of different lengths: a small curve for a jump length of 1, a medium curve for a jump length of 10, and a large curve for a jump length of 100. You can jump forward or backward.

For Example: **Jump from 0 to 26.**

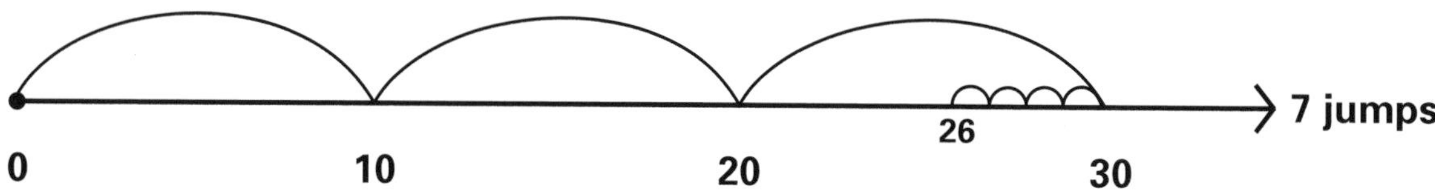

Complete Rounds 1 and 2 individually. After each round, write the total number of jumps you made next to each number line.

Round 1. Jump from 0 to 53.

0 ☐

Round 2. Jump from 0 to 29.

0 ☐

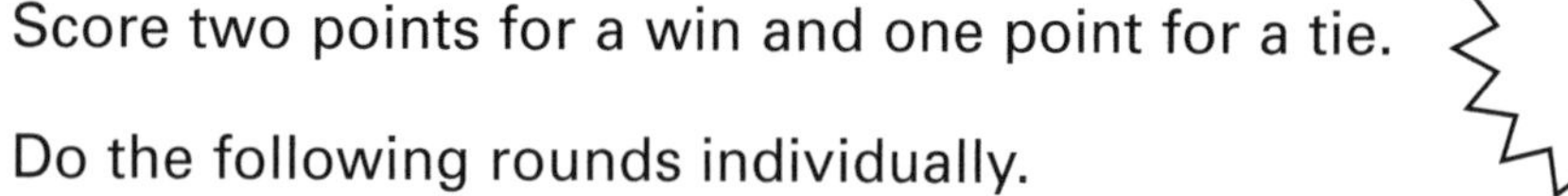

Compare your results with a partner.
Score two points for a win and one point for a tie.

SCORE (1–2)

Do the following rounds individually.

Round 3. Jump from 0 to 69.

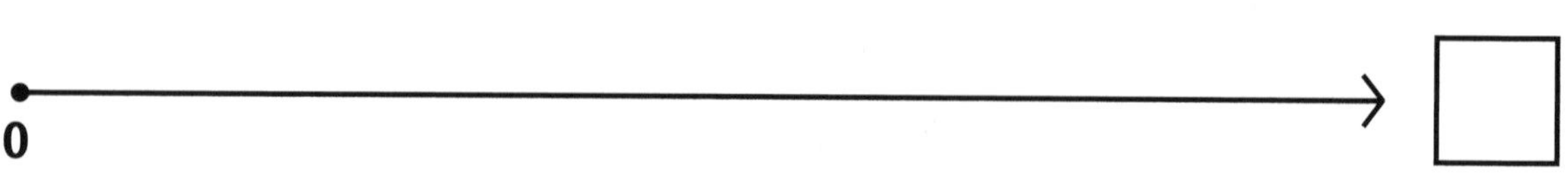

☐

Round 4. Jump from 0 to 83.

0 ☐

Name ______________________ Date__________ Class__________

Round 5. Jump from 0 to 57.

0

Compare your results with a partner.

Score two points for a win and one point for a tie.

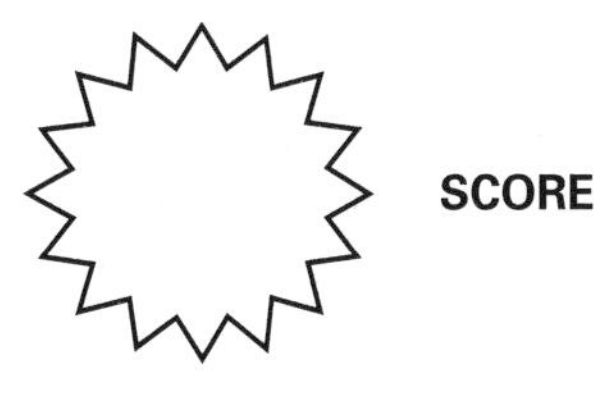

SCORE

The next few rounds are a little different Do them individually.

Round 6. Jump from 4 to 79.

Round 7. Jump from 45 to 87.

Round 8. Jump from 56 to 173.

Round 9. Jump from 324 to 546.

Round 10. Jump from 1492 to the current year.

Winner: ______________________

Winning Score: _______

TOTAL SCORE
(1–10)

Name ____________________ Date ____________ Class ____________

On the Number Line

A group of students has a paper airplane contest. The Distance List shows the flight distance for each person's airplane. The distance is measured along the ground in centimeters.

Distance List—Round 1	
Student	**Flight Distance (in cm)**
Jim	244
Shantha	367
Lester	120
Giorgio	167
Bido	250
Alice	203
Arba	278
Martha	385

1. Locate the numbers for the flight distances on this number line. Reasonable estimates will do.

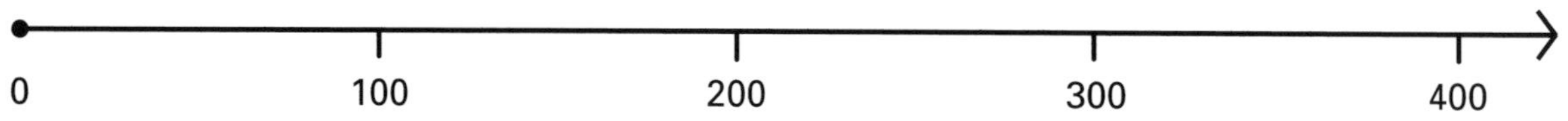

Length of Flight (in cm)

The students organized a second round. This number line shows the results of the second round.

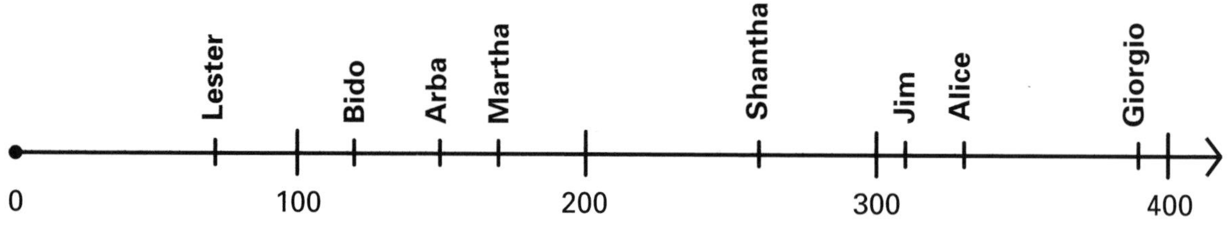

2. Use the number line to fill in the Distance List for Round 2. Reasonable estimates will do. Who is the winner after the second round? Explain how you decided.

Distance List—Round 2	
Student	**Flight Distance (in cm)**
Jim	______
Shantha	______
Lester	______
Giorgio	______
Bido	______
Alice	______
Arba	______
Martha	______

Name ______________________ Date ____________ Class ____________

The Number Line as a Tool (page 1)

Suppose you work at a booth selling beads. A customer wants to buy 29 brown beads and 67 amber-colored beads. All the beads sell for 10 cents each.

1. Find the total cost. Show your work.

2. There are different strategies to find the total number of beads. The number lines below show three strategies. Below each number line, describe the strategy shown.

a.

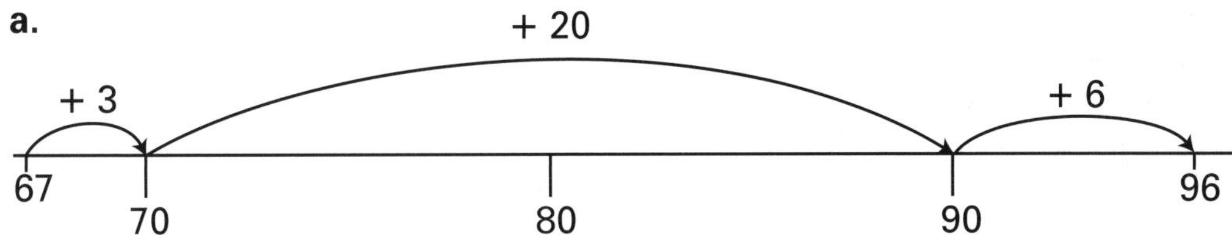

b.

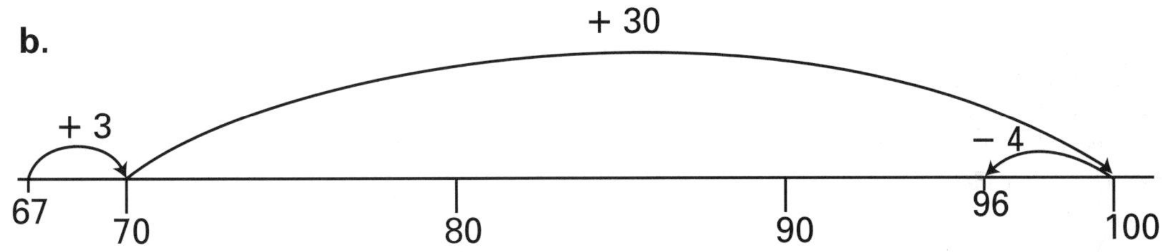

c.

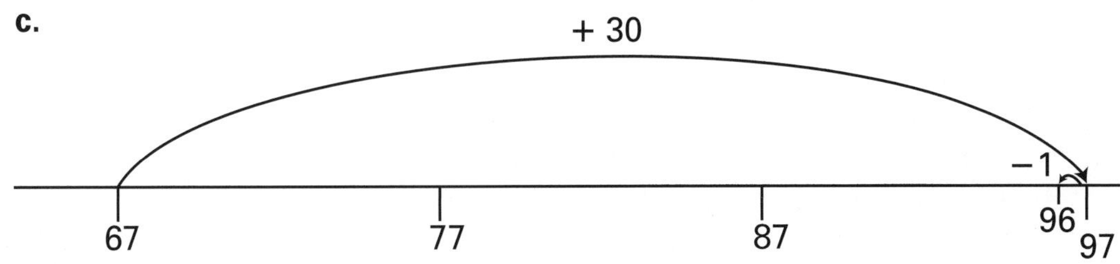

3. Use the number line below to show your strategy for adding 67 beads to 29 beads; start with 29 beads.

29

Name ______________________ Date ____________ Class ____________

The Number Line as a Tool (page 2)

Draw a number line to show how you would solve each problem mentally. Explain your solution.

Mira's necklace has 18 beads. Nancy's necklace has 75 beads more than Mira's.

4. How many beads does Nancy's necklace have?

Julie buys a package of beads for $2.10 and a cord for $0.98.

5. a. What is the total cost for Julie's items?

b. Julie pays with a 10-dollar bill. How much change does she receive?

Name ______________________ Date__________ Class__________

Each morning Hasan rides his bike 7.4 miles to school, and Jerret rides his bike 3.8 miles.

6. Compared to Jerret, how much farther does Hasan ride his bike to school?

Gwen and Gordon ride along a bike trail that is 36.4 miles long. Gwen's bike computer shows that they have already ridden their bikes 15.8 miles.

7. If they plan to ride the complete the trail, how many more miles will they ride their bikes?

Solve the following problems mentally. It may be helpful to make a mental model of the number line.

8. Jonathan is having a party for a few of his closest friends. The catering bill comes to $249. He decides to give a $38 tip. How much money does he give the caterers in total?

9. At a track meet, Lisa jumped 652 centimeters in the long jump competition, Shelice jumped 595 centimeters. Compared to Shelice, how much farther did Lisa jump?

10. Create and solve your own problem using the numbers 508 and 470.

Name ______________________ Date ____________ Class ____________

At the Cash Register

Imagine that you are the cashier at a store. Customers give you money to pay for their purchases. You have to give them change. When you make change, hand back the fewest bills and coins possible.

1. For each purchase, give change to each customer. Use tally marks to show how much of each coin and/or bill you would return to each customer. As an example, change for a purchase of $13.49 when the customer pays with a twenty-dollar bill is one penny, two quarters, one one-dollar bill, and one five-dollar bill.

Purchase	Payment	Change—Fewest Coin and Bills								
		1¢	5¢	10¢	25¢	$1	$5	$10	$20	$50
$13.49	$20.00	I			II	I	I			
$67.88	$100.00									
$198.21	$200.01									
$23.02	$100.02									

Now imagine that you are the customer.

2. For each purchase, write how much you would give a cashier. Then use tally marks to show how much of each coin/bill you expect as change.

Purchase	Payment	Change—Fewest Coin and Bills								
		1¢	5¢	10¢	25¢	$1	$5	$10	$20	$50
$5.98	$______									
$16.23	$______									
$59.80	$______									
$5.08	$______									

Name ______________________ Date ____________ Class ____________

How many quarters, dimes, and/or nickels do you have to put into this vending machine to get the following items? Record at least five possible coin combinations for each item. As an example, two of the five combinations for item **a** are listed in the table.

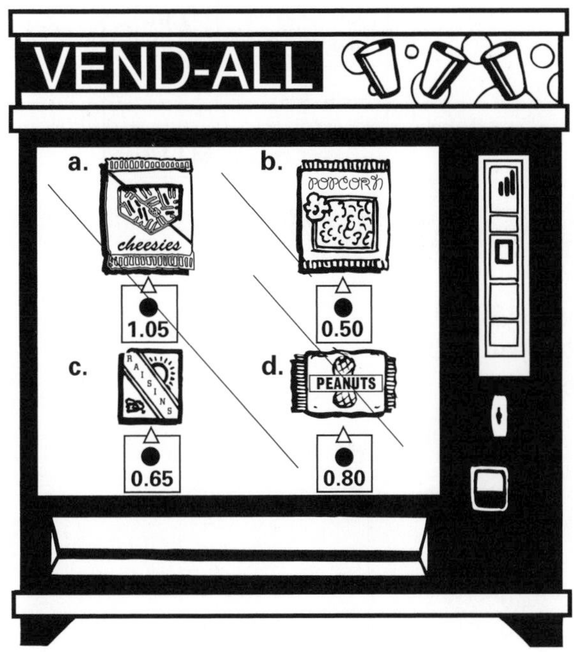

Five different possible coin combinations to Purchase each Item			
ITEM	quarters	dimes	nickels
a.	4	0	1
	2	5	1
	3	....	....
b.			
c.			
d.			

Name ________________ Date ________ Class ________

Checking the Bill

1. Patricia received this restaurant bill.

   After quickly checking the bill, Patricia knew the waiter made an addition error. Explain how she knew the addition was wrong even though she did not perform an exact calculation.

Check

	$6.98
	$7.98
	$4.25
	$6.96
	$2.00
	$3.00

Total $41.17

Thank You

2. Here are some receipts from shopping trips to the supermarket. Quickly estimate the total for each receipt and explain how you estimated.

a.	b.	c.	d.
$3.98	$2.97	$0.75	$0.24
$3.98	$3.06	$0.75	$0.24
$3.98	$5.99	$0.75	$0.24
$3.98	$0.99	$0.75	$0.24
$3.98		$0.75	$0.24
		$0.75	$0.24
		$0.75	$0.24
		$0.75	
Total ______	Total ______	Total ______	Total ______

d.	e.	f.	g.
$5.96	$5.98	$3.31	$6.38
$2.96	$9.02	$2.58	$4.12
$4.96	$6.97	$6.49	$9.72
$3.96	$3.03	$2.65	$4.08
$5.96	$4.02	$5.38	$5.74
	$2.98	$0.44	$2.68
Total ______	Total ______	Total ______	Total ______

3. Compare your estimates with a classmate. Describe a way you can improve your estimation skills.

Name ______________________ Date______________ Class______________

Collecting Pennies

Here is a penny-collecting tube. The tube is completely full when it contains 100 pennies ($1.00).

1. Draw a line to show the height of the tube if it contained each of these amounts of money. Write the corresponding letter next to each height. As an example, problem **a** has been done for you.

a. $0.25	**h.** $0.80
b. $0.50	**i.** $0.98
c. $0.75	**j.** $0.09
d. $0.20	**k.** $1.00
e. $0.02	**l.** $0.10
f. $0.77	**m.** $0.67
g. $0.40	

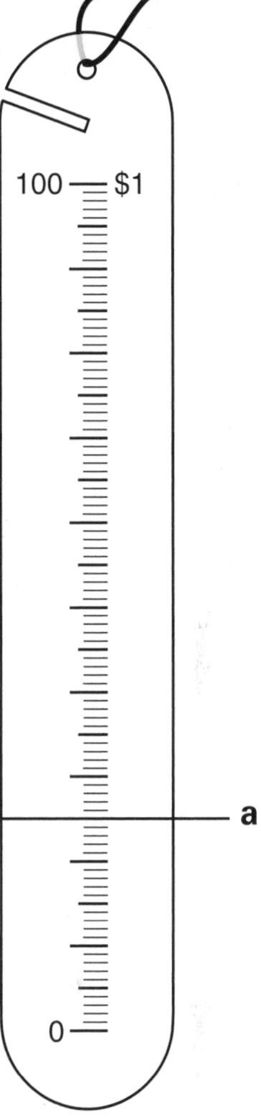

2. Draw an arrow to connect each decimal number to its unique place on the number line.

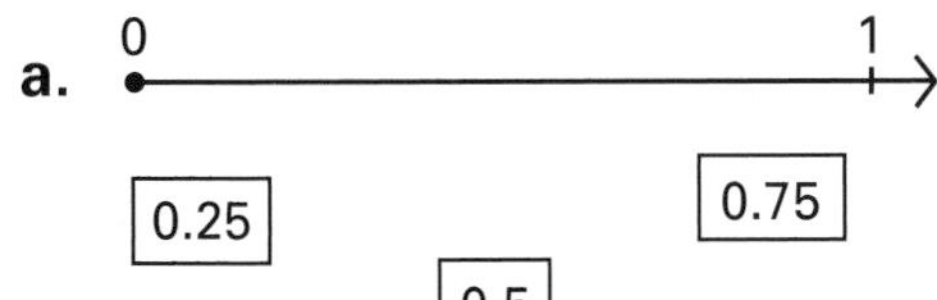

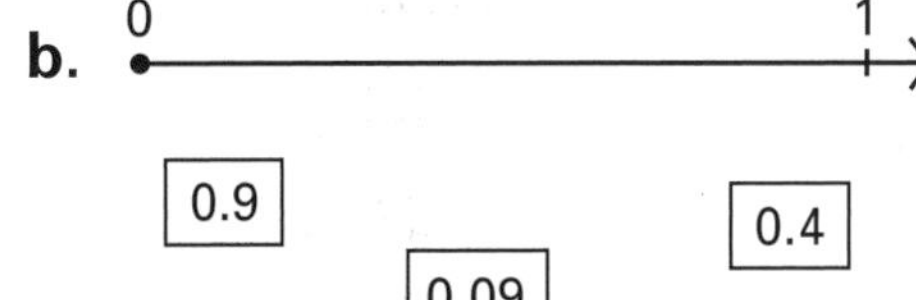

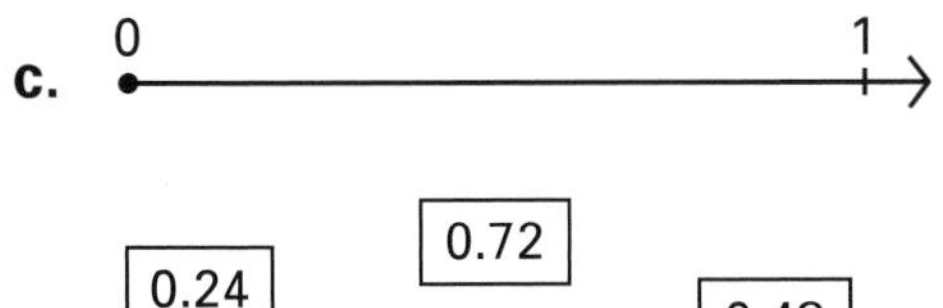

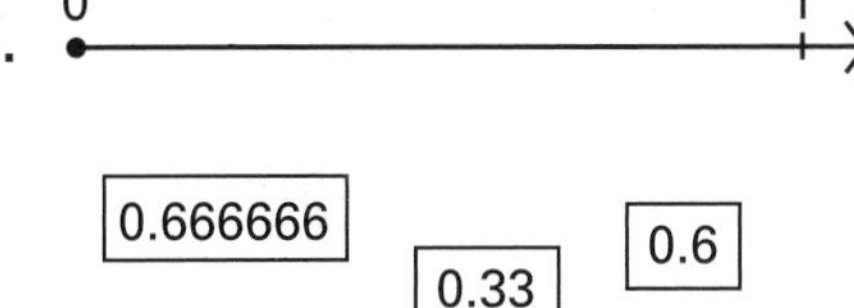

Name ______________________ Date __________ Class __________

Summer Camp

Ms. Lampert organizes a summer camp for children. This year, 169 children have signed up for camp. Ms. Lampert needs to figure out how many tents will accommodate 169 children. Each tent is large enough for 12 children.

1. a. How many tents does Ms. Lampert need? Solve the problem *without using a calculator.* Describe and label how you found your answer as Strategy 1.

b. Find a classmate who solved the problem using a different strategy. Copy this different strategy as Strategy 2.

This problem can be solved in many different ways. You might have written down all of the steps you took to find the answer. Using a **ratio table** is a good way to keep track of all the steps.

With a ratio table, you start with a known ratio (in this case, 1 tent for 12 children) and use it to find other numbers with the same ratio (10 tents for 120 children, for example). You can keep using the numbers you find to discover more numbers until you solve the problem.

Here is how Jamal solved this problem using a ratio table.

Tents	1	10	5	15	14
Children	12	120	60	180	168

2. Explain how Jamal found the numbers in each new column.

3. Explain how Jamal will use his ratio table to answer the question. (How many tents does Ms. Lampert need to accommodate 169 children?)

Name ______________________ Date ____________ Class ____________

Bottles (page 1)

1. Camp's juice cases contain 15 bottles of juice. Use the following ratio tables to find out how many bottles there are in different numbers of cases:

a. 8 cases

Cases	1	2	4	6				
Bottles	15							

b. 6 cases

Cases	1	2	3	6				
Bottles	15							

c. 15 cases

Cases	1	10	5	15				
Bottles	15							

d. 9 cases

Cases	1	10	9					
Bottles	15							

e. 99 cases

Cases	1							
Bottles	15							

2. Jake wants 155 bottles of Camp's juice. Use the following ratio table to determine how many cases he needs to order. Add more columns if necessary.

Cases	1							
Bottles	15							

Name ______________________ Date ____________ Class ____________

Bottles (page 2)

Camp's Beverages sells cases of mineral water and juice. A full case of mineral water contains 12 bottles.

3. Fill in this ratio table to find out how many bottles there are in 24 cases. (You do not have to use all columns in the table. You may add more columns if you need them.)

Cases	1						
Bottles	12						

Twenty-four cases of Camp's mineral water contain ______ bottles.

4. Use the ratio table to find out how many bottles there are in 31 cases.

(You may add more columns if you need them. On the other hand, you may leave columns blank if you do not need them.)

Cases	1						
Bottles	12						

Thirty-one cases of Camp's mineral water contain ______ bottles.

5. Jake wants 98 bottles of mineral water for an office party. How many cases will he order?

Cases	1						
Bottles	12						

For Jake's order of 98 bottles, he will order ______ cases of Camp's mineral water.

Name ______________________ Date ____________ Class ____________

How Do You Do It? (page 1)

Using ratio tables is a convenient way to solve some problems. You may have discovered that the ratio table offers a handy way to write down the intermediate steps you take to solve a problem.

There are several ways to use existing numbers to find new numbers. Here are some examples of operations you can use.

1. Fill in the missing numbers.

a. Doubling or Multiplying by Two

× 2 × 2

Cases	1	2	4
Bottles	15		

× 2 × 2

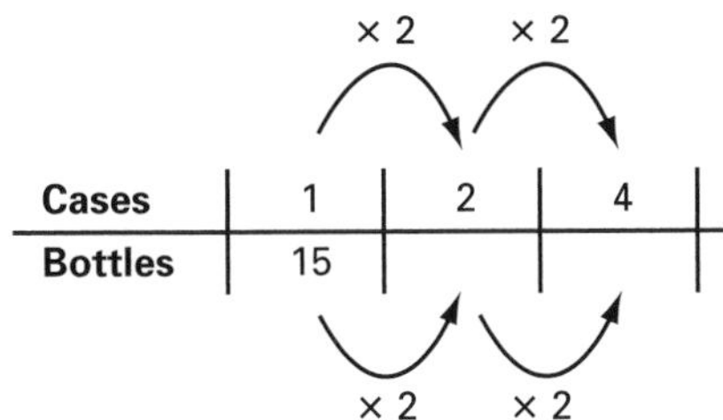

b. Halving or Dividing By Two

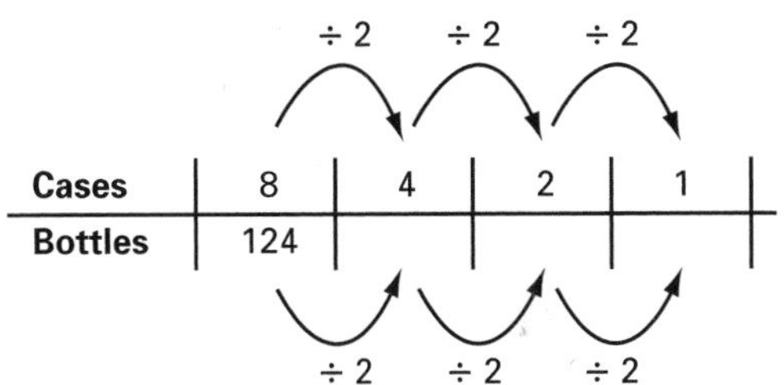

÷ 2 ÷ 2 ÷ 2

Cases	8	4	2	1
Bottles	124			

÷ 2 ÷ 2 ÷ 2

c. Times Ten

× 10

Cases	1		
Bottles	15		

× 10

d. Multiplying

× 2 × 5

Cases	1		
Bottles	15		

× 2 × 5

e. Dividing

÷ 10 ÷ 9

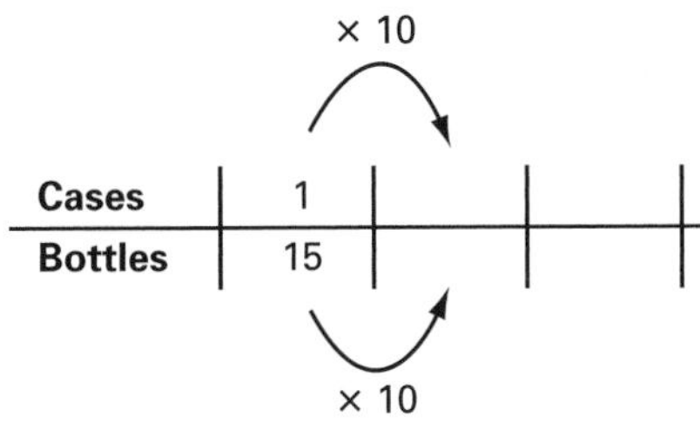

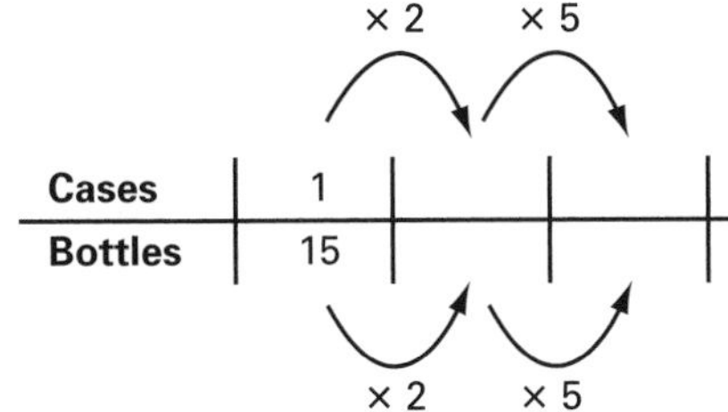

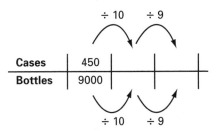

Cases	450		
Bottles	9000		

÷ 10 ÷ 9

f. Adding Columns

× 10 + column 1

Cases	1	10	11
Bottles	12	120	

× 10 + column 1

g. Subtracting Columns

× 10 – column 1

Cases	1	10	9
Bottles	12	120	

× 10 – column 1

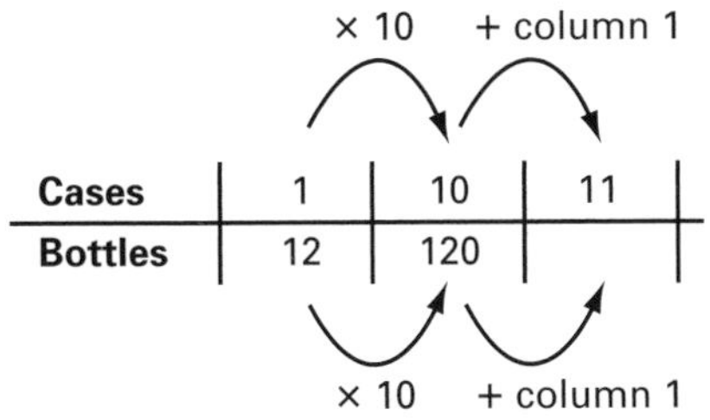

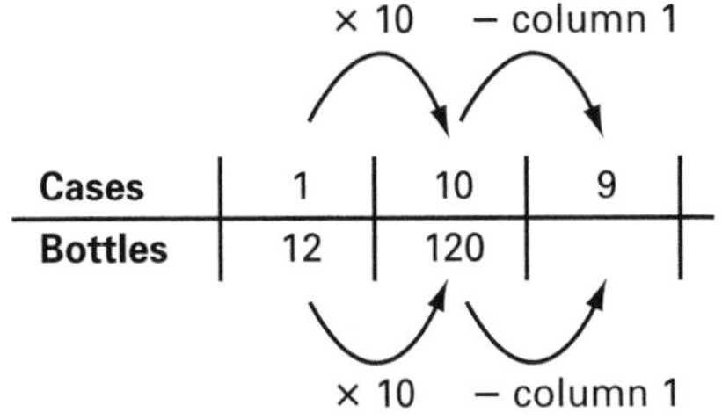

Name ________________ Date ________ Class ________

How Do You Do It? (page 2)

Finish the ratio tables below. Circle the operation you used.

2. Anton earns $13 a day at his summer job, baby-sitting his cousins. How much will he earn in 20 days?

Days	1	10	20
Dollars	13	130	

adding • times 10 • doubling
halving • subtracting
multiplying

3. One bottle of apple juice costs $2.75. How much do four bottles of apple juice cost?

Bottles	1	2	4
Dollars	2.75	5.50	

adding • times 10 • doubling
halving • subtracting
multiplying

4. Mr. Pink wants to buy 40 stamps for his office. How much will he pay if each stamp is worth $0.37?

Stamps	1	2	4	40
Dollars	0.37	0.74	1.48	

adding • times 10 • doubling
halving • subtracting
multiplying

5. Altagracia can fill six glasses with one bottle of apple juice. How many glasses can she fill with three bottles?

Bottles	1	3	
Glasses	6		

adding • times 10 • doubling
halving • subtracting
multiplying

On your own:

6. There are 24 bottles in one case. How many bottles are there in nine cases?

Cases	1							
Bottles	24							

Name ______________________ Date______________ Class____________

Plants I

Two geranium plants cost \$1.25.

1. How many plants can you buy for ten dollars?
Show your work.

Here you see how Nadia solved the problem.
She made a mistake somewhere.

Nadia

Plants	2	4	6	8
Dollars	1.25	2.50	5.00	10.00

You can buy eight plants for ten dollars.

2. a. Check each step Nadia made in the ratio table and find where she made the mistake. Then correct her work.

b. How would you explain to Nadia what she did wrong?

Theo solved the following problem:
Three violets cost \$1.75. What will 15 violets cost?

Theo

Plants	3	6	12	15
Dollars	1.75	3.50	7.00	10.00

15 violets will cost ten dollars.

Theo also did something wrong.

3. a. Find where he made the mistake and correct his work.

b. How would you explain to Theo what he did wrong?

Name ______________________ Date ____________ Class ____________

Plants II (page 1)

Mr. Martin's biology class is starting a school garden. They will be ordering plants by the box from a nursery. Mr. Martin asked the class to figure out how many tomato plants are in 16 boxes if one box contains 35 plants.

Three students—Darrell, Tasha, and Carla—solved the problem using ratio tables, but each student used a different table.

1. Darrell solved the problem as shown below. Explain Darrell's solution.

Boxes	1	2	3	4	5	6	7	8	16
Plants	35	70	105	140	175	210	245	280	560

2. Tasha solved the problem as shown below. Explain Tasha's solution.

Boxes	1	2	4	8	16
Plants	35	70	140	280	560

3. Carla solved the problem as shown below. Explain Carla's solution.

Boxes	1	10	2	6	16
Plants	35	350	70	210	560

4. Think of your own way to use a ratio table to figure out how many tomato plants are in 16 boxes with 35 tomato plants in each box. Show your solution in the table below. You may add as many columns as you need to the table.

Boxes	1					
Tomato Plants	35					

5. Cactus plants are shipped 45 pots to a box. If Mr. Martin's class orders 360 cactus plants, how many boxes will they get? Show your strategy using the following ratio table.

Boxes						
Cactuses						

6. Mr. Martin's students decide that they need 675 cactus plants. How many boxes will arrive?

Boxes						
Cactuses						

7. Rose bushes are shipped in boxes of 15. Mr. Martin's class orders 255 rose bushes. How many boxes is this?

Boxes					
Roses					

8. Strawberry plants are shipped in boxes of 70. If Mr. Martin's class orders 980 strawberry plants, how many boxes will arrive?

Boxes					
Strawberry Plants					

Name ______________________ Date ____________ Class ____________

Fruits

In order to solve the problems on this page, you may use the ratio table given with each problem. If necessary, add extra columns.

1. A fruit stand sells three apples for $2. How much would you have to pay for 12 apples?

Apples	3			
Dollars	2.00			

2. What would you have to pay for 33 apples? Choose your own method to calculate the answer.

Apples	3					
Dollars	2.00					

3. The fruit stand sells five California oranges for $3.75. How much would you have to pay for 35 oranges?

Oranges	5			
Dollars	3.75			

4. Four Florida oranges sell for $2.50. You have $10 to spend. How many oranges can you buy?

Oranges	4			
Dollars	2.50			

5. Two cantaloupes sell for $3. How many cantaloupes can you buy for $7.50?

Cantaloupes	2			
Dollars	3.00			

Name ________________________ Date ____________ Class ____________

Two Steps for Efficiency (page 1)

1. Find the answers to the following problems without using a pencil and paper or a calculator.

a. 547 + 99 =

b. 437 + 99 =

c. 8,035 + 99 =

d. 63 + 99 =

e. 21,653 + 99 =

2. Did you discover any shortcuts when you solved problem 1? If so, explain; if not, look back and write about one you could have used.

Karen has $483 in her savings account. She deposits another $90 into her account and then figures out her total balance.

The arrow string below shows Karen's method.

First I added 100 to 483, which gives me 583. But I added too much, so then I subtracted 10 from 583. The answer is $573.

$483 \xrightarrow{+100} 583 \xrightarrow{-10} 573$

3. Rewrite the following problems as arrow strings and then solve them. Each arrow string should use Karen's method to make the calculation easier to do mentally.

a. 56 + 28 =

b. 327 + 51 =

c. 956 + 98 =

Name _______________________________ Date______________ Class____________

Two Steps for Efficiency (page 2)

When you choose an appropriate strategy, some subtraction problems become easy too. For example 465 – 37.

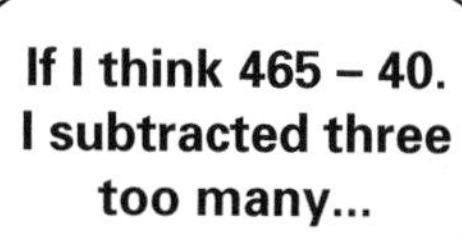
If I think 465 – 40.
I subtracted three
too many...

So I have to add
three at the end to
make up for taking
away too many.

You can use arrow strings to show this strategy:

$465 \xrightarrow{-40}$ ____ $\xrightarrow{+3}$ ____

4. Fill in the blanks.

Solve the following subtraction problems mentally. Use arrow strings to show what strategy you used.

5. a. 743 – 92 =

b. 132 – 85 =

c. 578 – 99 =

d. 1643 – 75 =

Name ______________________ Date ____________ Class ____________

Make It Easy

1. Solve the following addition and subtraction problems mentally. Use arrow strings to show what strategy you used.

a. 624 + 99 =

b. 624 − 99 =

c. 5,444 + 999 =

d. 5,444 − 999 =

e. 832 + 90 =

f. 832 − 90 =

g. 1,573 + 98 =

h. 1,573 − 98 =

i. 365 + 997 =

j. 4,526 − 997 =

k. 6,000 − 991 =

l. 5,001 + 998 =

Name ______________________ Date ____________ Class ____________

Recipes (page 1)

Banana Shake

4 servings:

2 bananas

$\frac{1}{3}$ cup lemon juice

$\frac{1}{4}$ cup granulated sugar

$\frac{1}{2}$ quart milk

1 cup vanilla ice cream

Blend until smooth.

Tanisha's favorite summertime drink is a banana shake. She started the following chart so she would know how to make the shake when different numbers of guests join her. Help Tanisha by filling in her chart.

Servings	**4**	**8**		**6**			
Bananas	2		1		6		
Lemon Juice (cups)	$\frac{1}{3}$						$\frac{1}{12}$
Sugar (cups)	$\frac{1}{4}$						
Milk (quarts)	$\frac{1}{2}$					2	
Ice Cream (cups)	1		$\frac{1}{2}$		3		$\frac{1}{4}$

Name ______________________ Date__________ Class__________

Strawberry Punch

8 servings:

$\frac{2}{3}$ cup lemon juice

$\frac{1}{4}$ cup granulated sugar

$1\frac{1}{3}$ cups strawberries, sliced

4 cups ginger ale

16 ice cubes

Stir ingredients together in a punch bowl.

Alonzo likes to make punch for his friends on a hot summer day. He started the following chart so he will know how to make strawberry punch when guests join him. Help Alonzo by filling in the rest of his chart.

Servings	8	4	16		20			
Lemon Juice (cups)	$\frac{2}{3}$			2				
Sugar (cups)	$\frac{1}{4}$						$1\frac{1}{4}$	
Strawberries (cups)	$1\frac{1}{3}$					2		
Ginger Ale (cups)	4							18
Ice Cubes	16							

Name ______________________ Date ____________ Class ____________

East of Yaksee Cave (page 1)

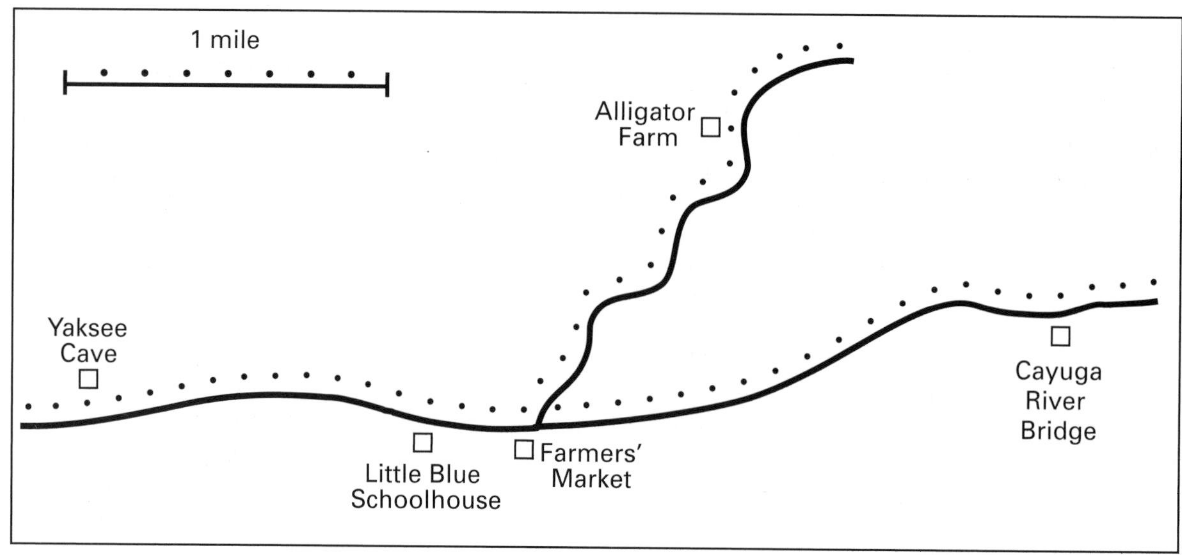

1. There is a scale line on the map. What information can you use from this scale line?

Here is a distance table for this map. Distances from the Little Blue Schoolhouse are along the first row. For example, it is $\frac{3}{8}$ of a mile from the Schoolhouse to the Farmers' Market.

	Little Blue Schoolhouse	Yaksee Cave	Farmers' Market	Alligator Farm	Cayuga River Bridge
Little Blue Schoolhouse	0	$\frac{7}{8}$ mile	$\frac{3}{8}$ mile	$1\frac{7}{8}$ miles	2 miles
Yaksee Cave					
Farmers' Market					
Alligator Farm					
Cayuga River Bridge					

2. Use the map to fill in the rest of the distance table. Whenever possible, express the fractional distances as halves or quarters instead of eighths of a mile.

Name ______________________ Date ____________ Class ____________

East of Yaksee Cave (page 2)

A new sign will be placed at the intersection near the Farmers' Market.

This sign will have information about distances expressed in miles and in minutes walking. Expressing distance in time is helpful for visitors.

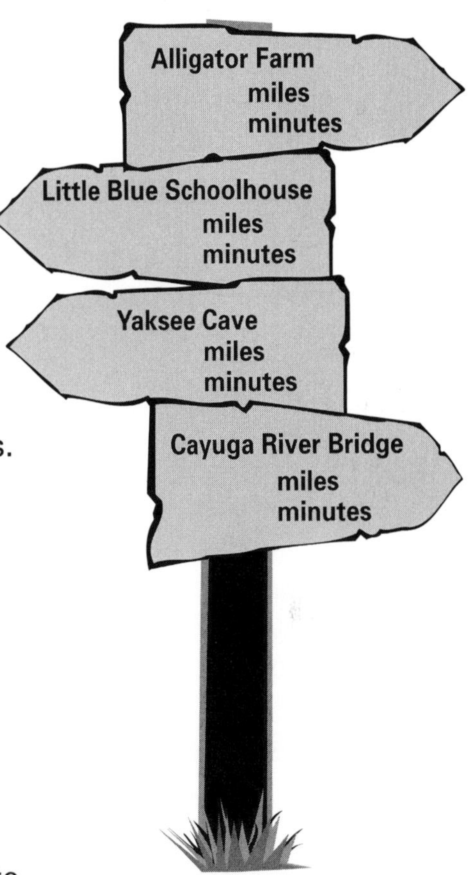

3. Use your previous work with Yaksee Cave to fill in the mile distances on the sign.

To calculate the distances in minutes walking, you can use a double scale line with miles and minutes. It takes about 60 minutes to walk 2 miles.

4. Use the double scale line to estimate the minute distances on the sign. Complete the sign.

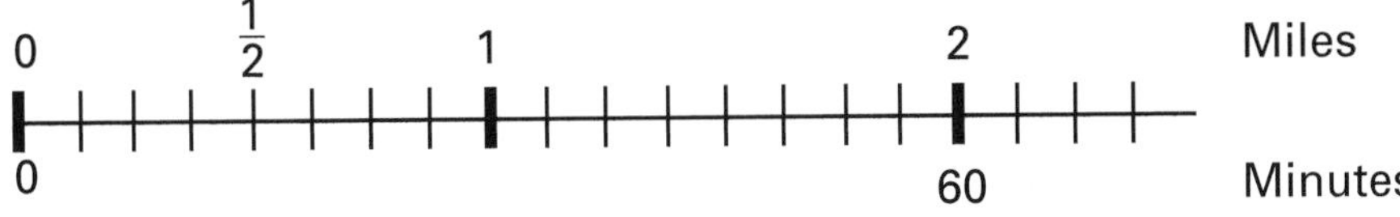

Name ____________________ Date ____________ Class ____________

Passing by Tom's House

Here is a map of the area near Tom's house. This map does not show a scale line.

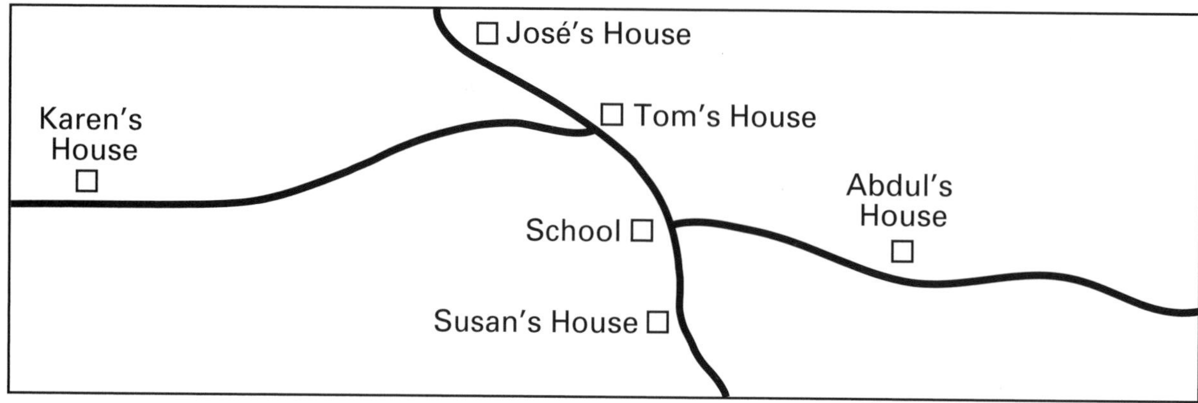

The distances on the map are to scale. To use this map, you can use the information in the first row of the distance table below. It shows the distance from the school to each person's home.

	School	Tom	José	Karen	Abdul	Susan
School	0	$\frac{3}{4}$ mi	$1\frac{1}{2}$ mi	3 mi	$1\frac{1}{8}$ mi	$\frac{5}{8}$ mi
Tom						
José						
Karen						
Abdul						
Susan						

1. Fill in the rest of the distance table. Whenever possible, express the distances as halves or quarters instead of eighths of a mile.

You can write a subtraction number sentence to represent distances. For example, the distance from Tom's house to José's is $1\frac{1}{2} - \frac{3}{4} = \frac{3}{4}$.

2. Use the distance information to write six number sentences using both addition and subtraction.

Name ______________________ Date ____________ Class ____________

Driving to Mons

The town of Mons is close to five other cities.

This map shows the driving distance from Mons to each of the nearby cities. The distance is expressed in hours.

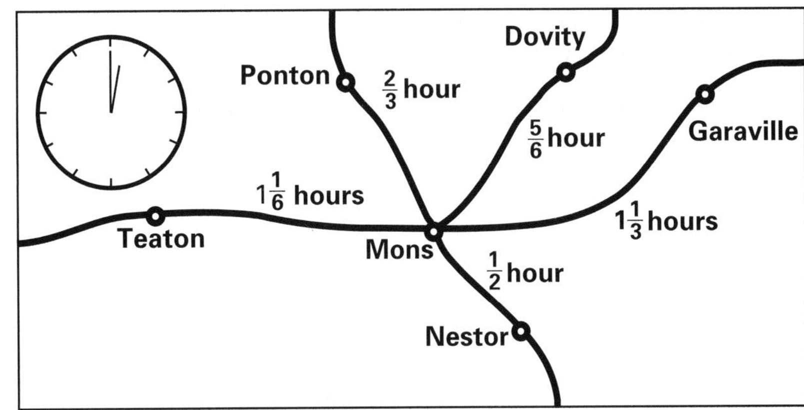

Here is a driving distance table for the cities near Mons. The map information is recorded in the table as hours and minutes. For example, the distance from Mons to Ponton is $\frac{2}{3}$ of an hour. In the table, it is recorded as 40 minutes.

	Mons	Ponton	Dovity	Garaville	Nestor	Teaton
Mons	0	40 min	50 min	1 hr 20 min	30 min	1 hr 10 min
Ponton						
Dovity						
Garaville						
Nestor						
Teaton						

1. Fill in the rest of the distance table.
2. To drive from Ponton to Dovity, you need $\frac{2}{3}$ hour + $\frac{5}{6}$ hour.
   a. What time did you enter in your table?
   b. Use your answer to problem **a** to explain that $\frac{2}{3} + \frac{5}{6} = 1\frac{1}{2}$.
3. a. How many hours and minutes is $\frac{1}{2}$ hr + $1\frac{1}{3}$ hrs?
   b. Use your answer to problem a. to explain that $\frac{1}{2} + 1\frac{1}{3} = 1\frac{5}{6}$.
4. Solve the following addition problems. It may be helpful to think of hours and minutes.

   a. $\frac{1}{3} + 1\frac{1}{6}$ b. $\frac{1}{2} + \frac{1}{6}$

Name ______________________ Date ____________ Class ____________

Sisters (page 1)

Ms. Nakamura's students take a survey and discover that $\frac{1}{2}$ of the students in the class have only one sister and $\frac{1}{3}$ have more than one sister. The class displays the survey results in the pie chart.

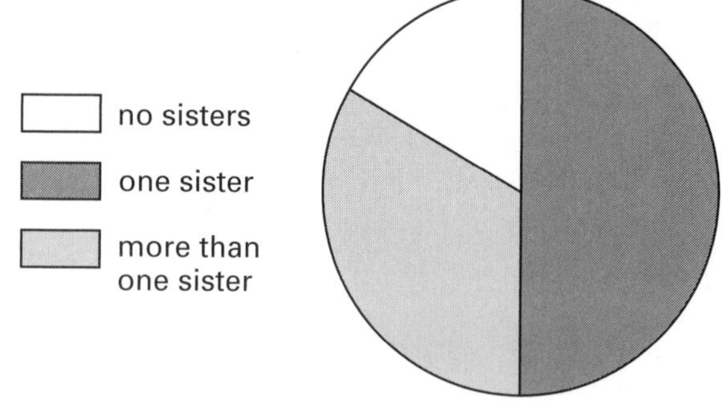

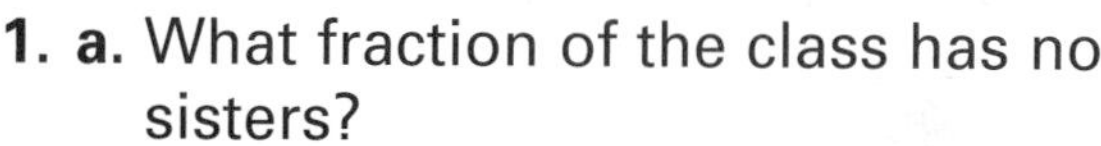

1. **a.** What fraction of the class has no sisters?

   b. What fraction of the class has one or more sisters?

   c. Can it be possible that there were 20 students involved in the survey? Explain why or why not.

Mr. Brown's class conducted the same survey. Twenty-four students were involved in this survey. Six students had only one sister, and four students had more than one sister.

To display the survey results, you can make a pie chart, but you also can use a segmented bar.

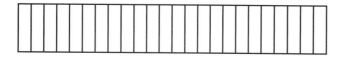

On this bar with twenty-four segments, each segment represents one student.

2. **a.** Use colors to display the survey results for Mr. Brown's class.

   b. What fraction of the class has one sister or more?

   c. What fraction of the class has no sister? Explain your answer.

3. Is it possible to display the survey results of this survey on a bar with only twelve segments? Explain why or why not.

Name ______________________ Date ____________ Class ____________

Sisters (page 2)

If you want to add fractions with different denominators, you can make bars, each with the same number of segments, to represent the fractions. For example, $\frac{1}{4} + \frac{1}{6}$ can be solved by using two bars with 12 segments each.

$\frac{1}{4}$ of 12 segments is three segments.

$\frac{1}{6}$ of 12 segments is two segments.

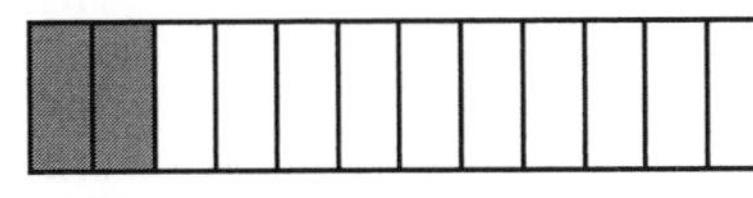

The total is five out of twelve segments:

$$\frac{1}{4} + \frac{1}{6} = \frac{3}{12} + \frac{2}{12}$$
$$= \frac{5}{12}$$

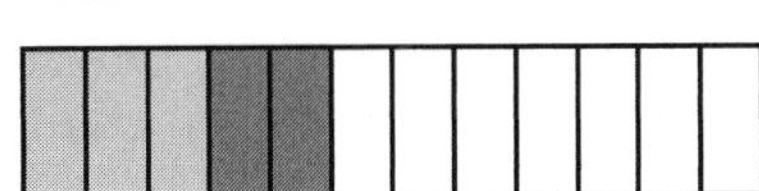

4. Explain why you could also use two bars with 24 segments each to add $\frac{1}{4}$ and $\frac{1}{6}$.

5. Solve the following addition problems. If necessary, make two bars, each with the same number of segments, to represent the two fractions.

a. $\frac{1}{4} + \frac{1}{8} =$

b. $\frac{2}{3} + \frac{1}{4} =$

c. $\frac{1}{2} + \frac{1}{6} =$

d. $\frac{1}{6} + \frac{4}{9} =$

e. $\frac{1}{10} + \frac{3}{4} =$

f. $\frac{3}{8} + \frac{1}{2} =$

g. $\frac{1}{3} + \frac{1}{5} =$

h. $\frac{2}{6} + \frac{1}{4} =$

i. $\frac{2}{4} + \frac{3}{10} =$

Name ______________________ Date ____________ Class ____________

School Plays

The high school Drama Club produced seven plays last year in different places around town. Some of the plays were more popular than other plays. The club kept track of attendance using the percent bars.

For each play, fill in the information to express the attendance as a fraction, as a percent, and as the number of seats occupied.

1. 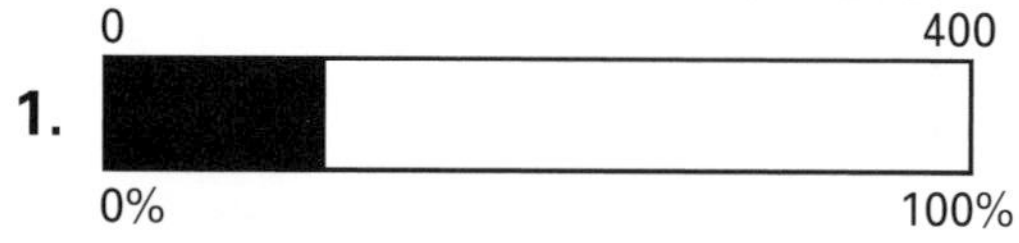

Fraction occupied: _______
Percent occupied: _______
Seats occupied: _______

2. 

Fraction occupied: _______
Percent occupied: _______
Seats occupied: _______

3. 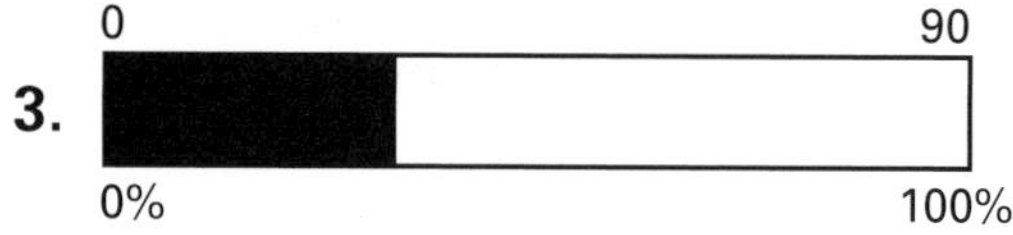

Fraction occupied: _______
Percent occupied: _______
Seats occupied: _______

4. 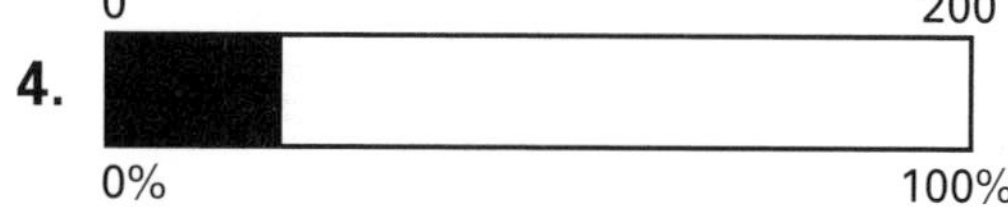

Fraction occupied: _______
Percent occupied: _______
Seats occupied: _______

5. 

Fraction occupied: _______
Percent occupied: _______
Seats occupied: _______

6. 

Fraction occupied: _______
Percent occupied: _______
Seats occupied: _______

7. 

Fraction occupied: _______
Percent occupied: _______
Seats occupied: _______

here is a great rivalry between the sports teams of East Middle School and West Middle School.

1. At the last basketball game between East and West, there were 160 East fans and 240 West fans. The sports writer for the East Middle School newspaper wanted to report the percentages of fans for each school.

   a. Fill in this ratio table to account for a total of 100 spectators.

East Fans	160				
West Fans	240				
Total Fans	400				

   b. What percent of the fans at the basketball game were East fans? And the percentage of West fans?

   c. What was the ratio of East fans to West fans? Write this ratio in simplest form using the smallest whole numbers but keeping the ratio intact.

2. At the last gymnastics meet between the two schools, the ratio of East fans to West fans was 13 to 7.

   a. What percent of the fans at the gymnastic meet were East fans? And the percentage of West fans?

East Fans					
West Fans					
Total Fans					

   b. Shade and label the following percent bars to show the percentages of East fans and West fans.

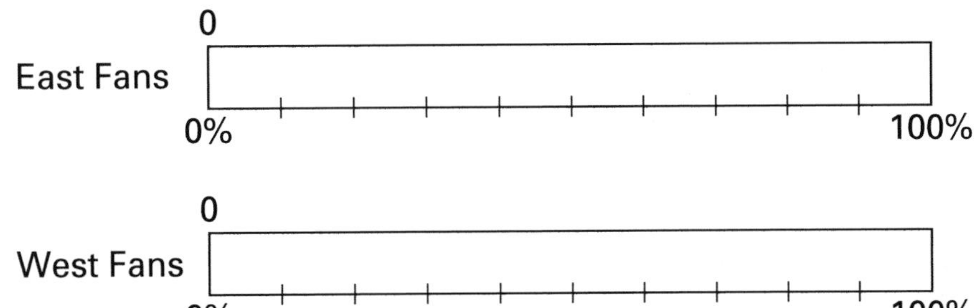

   c. There were 180 fans at the gymnastics meet. Use either a percent bar or a ratio table to find the number of fans for each team.

Per 100 (page 2)

3. At the last swim meet between the two schools, there were only 28 East fans and 220 West fans.

What percent of the fans at the swim meet were East fans? And the percentage of West fans? Show your strategy.

4. a. At which of the sporting events mentioned in problems 1–3 did East Middle School have the highest percentage of fans?

b. At which sporting event did East Middle School have the most fans?

Name ______________________ Date______________ Class____________

From Ratios to Percents (page 1)

Here are two methods you can use to convert a ratio into a percent.

- The Ratio Method: Use a ratio table to calculate how many per 100.
- The Fraction Method: Rewrite the ratio as a fraction and then use the relationship between fractions, decimals, and percents.

1. Two out of five students have read *The Hobbit*. Use each of the methods described above to find a percent equivalent to the ratio two out of five.

Ratio Table Method:

Part						
Whole						

Fraction Method:

2. Two out of three students have read *The Diary of Anne Frank*. Use each of the methods described above to find a percent equivalent to the ratio two out of three.

Ratio Table Method:

Part						
Whole						

Fraction Method:

Name ______________________ Date ____________ Class ____________

From Ratios to Percents (page 2)

3. Find an equivalent percent for each of the following. Use any method, but show your work.

a. Three out of 20 students participate in the Drama Club.

b. Seven out of 10 students have a bicycle.

c. Three out of four students have read *A Wrinkle in Time*.

d. Three out of eight students have read *The Outsiders*.

e. One out of three students has read *Roll of Thunder, Hear My Cry*.

f. Eight out of 12 students have seen the movie *Jurassic Park*.

g. Only one out of 12 students has read the book on which the movie *Jurassic Park* was based.

h. The school has 250 students, but five are not in school today.

i. Mrs. Robinson's class has 14 girls and 11 boys.

Name ______________________ Date ____________ Class ____________

Tipping

1. Ms. Eng usually gives a 10% tip in restaurants. Mr. Lonetree usually gives a 15% tip. Fill in the tip table below, to show what Ms. Eng and Mr. Lonetree would leave for a tip.

Restaurant	Bill	10% Tip	15% Tip
Hamburger Heaven	$13.65		
The Apple Dumplin' Diner	$ 7.42		
Frank's Pizza Palace	$29.10		
The Newton Grill	$52.85		
Chez Louis	$77.50		

2. Decide whether Ms. Eng or Mr. Lonetree left the given tip for each of the following bills. Explain your choice.

Total Bill **Tip**

a. $32.08   

b. $27.27    

c. $ 8.32  

d. $14.00  

e. $19.58   

Name ______________________ Date ____________ Class ____________

Map It Out!

What comes to mind when you see $\frac{1}{4}$? Make a mental map of the many different meanings for $\frac{1}{4}$ by filling in the boxes around $\frac{1}{4}$. You may draw additional boxes if you need them. After you finish, work with a partner to make a poster for the mental map of $\frac{1}{4}$.

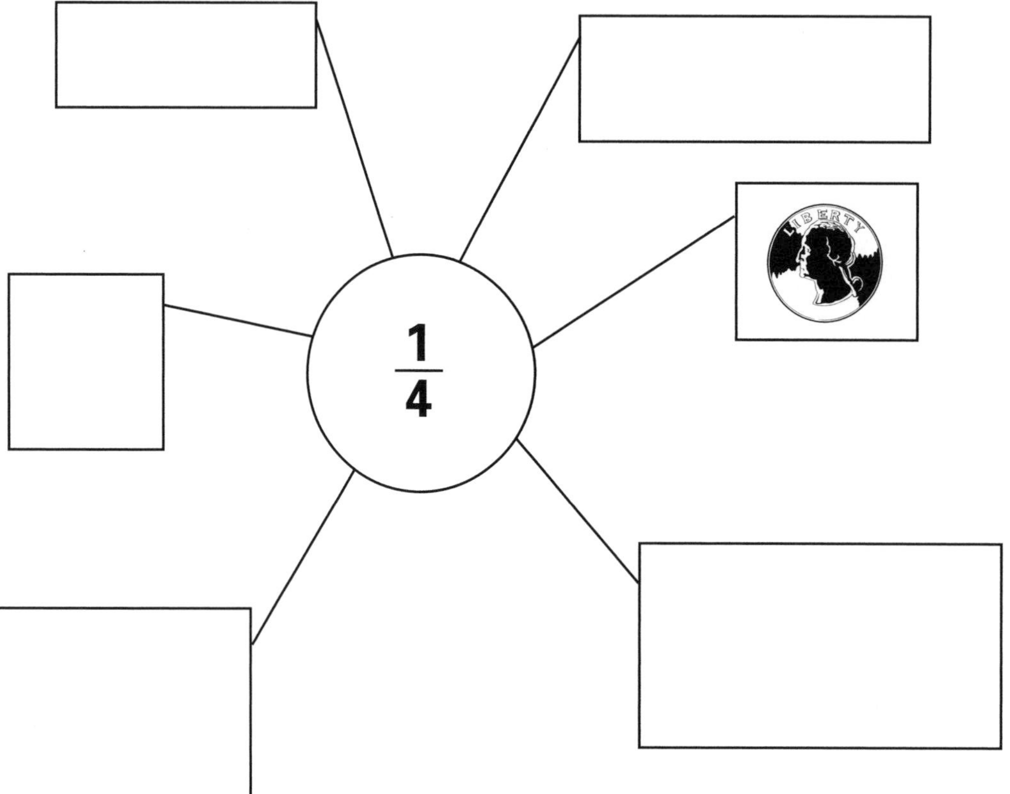

Name ______________________ Date ____________ Class ____________

Number Sentences

Sandra, Barbara, and Vito create number sentences. They choose a target number and create number sentences using the four operations + − × ÷ and any of these numbers: **100 25 10 5 1**.

They decide to use the numbers only once, but it is not necessary to use all of the numbers.

They decide to use **( )**, but not a calculator.

Here is their work for a target number of 750.

(100 − 25) × 10 = 750 Sandra

(10 × 5 + 25) × 100 = 750 Barbara

5 × 100 + 10 × 25 = 750 Vito

1. Who has a correct number sentence?

2. Create three different number sentences for each target.

a. Target is 1,500.

b. Target is 300.

c. Target is 535.

Name ______________________ Date ____________ Class ____________

Too High, Too Low

Too High, Too Low

This is a game for two players.

- Player 1 secretly writes a decimal number between 0 and 10. The decimal number can be up through the tenths (one decimal place). Keep this number out of the other player's sight!
- Player 2 tries to guess the number.
- Player 1 responds that the guess is "Too high" or "Too low."
- Play continues until Player 2 guesses the number. Player 1 should keep a record of the number of guesses needed!
- Change roles and play again. The player who uses the least number of guesses wins the game.

Variations on this game:

- Choose a decimal number between 0 and −10. (Think of temperatures on a thermometer.)
- Choose a decimal number between 0 and 10, but the decimal number can be up through hundredths (two decimal places).

Name ______________________ Date ____________ Class ____________

Climbers who reach the top of Mt. Erghoog earn a certificate.

The park station keeps many certificates on hand because Mt. Erghoog is a very popular mountain to climb.

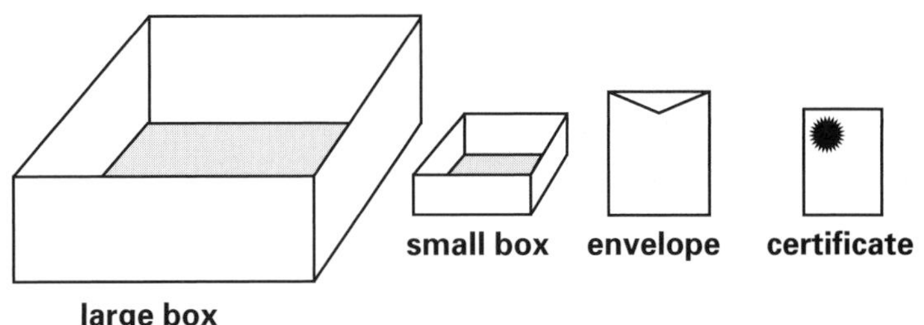

Certificates are shipped to the park station in large boxes.

Each large box contains 10 small boxes.

Inside each small box are 10 envelopes.

Inside each envelope are 10 certificates.

Raúl regularly takes inventory of the certificates to make sure they do not run out!

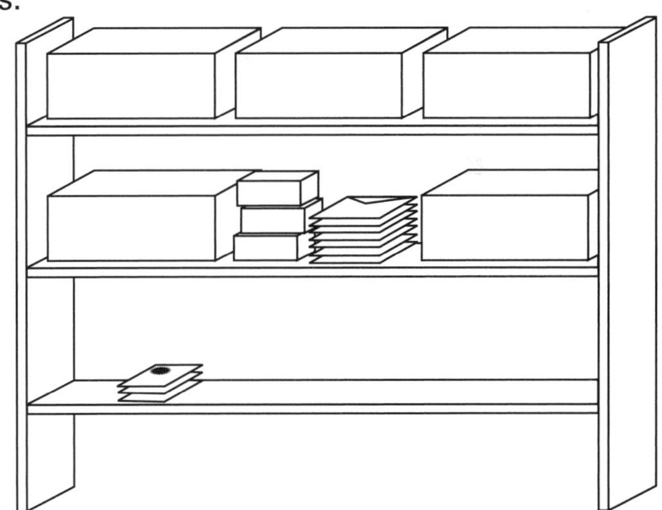

On May 1, here is what Raúl sees on the shelf. There are three loose certificates on the bottom shelf, and all the boxes and envelopes are full.

1. Help Raúl record the inventory by filling in this table.

Date	Large Boxes	Small Boxes	Envelopes	Certificates
May 1				

2. How many certificates were in stock on May 1?

Name ______________________ Date ____________ Class ____________

Certificates (page 2)

3. Raúl took the inventory again on July 1. There were 29 large boxes, 16 small boxes, 8 envelopes, and 29 loose certificates. According to the computer, there should have been 30,709 certificates in stock. Was the actual number of certificates in agreement with the computer? Explain.

4. After one busy weekend, the shelf was in disarray. The workers opened too many boxes and envelopes unnecessarily. Here is what was on the shelf.

Large Boxes	Small Boxes	Envelopes	Certificates
21	19	48	38

Put the shelf back in order so that it would be easy to take inventory.

Large Boxes	Small Boxes	Envelopes	Certificates

5. On September 1, there are 2,015 certificates on the shelf. Fill in the table to show different ways the shelf might be organized.

Large Boxes	Small Boxes	Envelopes	Certificates

Name ________________________ Date ____________ Class ____________

Close Enough

Draw a circle around the number closest to the correct answer. Do not use your calculator or make precise calculations. Write a short explanation of how you made your selection.

1. 101 × 11 =

800

900

1,000

1,100

1,200

2. 391 × 391 =

10

100

1,000

10,000

100,000

1,000,000

3. 111 × 909 =

800

9,000

10,000

110,000

1,200,000

4. 91 × 19 × 19 =

500

5,000

50,000

500,000

5,000,000

5. 30 × 41 × 52 =

100

1,000

10,000

100,000

1,000,000

6. 1,234 × 5,678 =

1,000

10,000

100,000

1,000,000

10,000,000

Name ______________________ Date ______________ Class ____________

Rearrangements

How much money is 12 quarters? Study the pictures and you will find an easy solution.

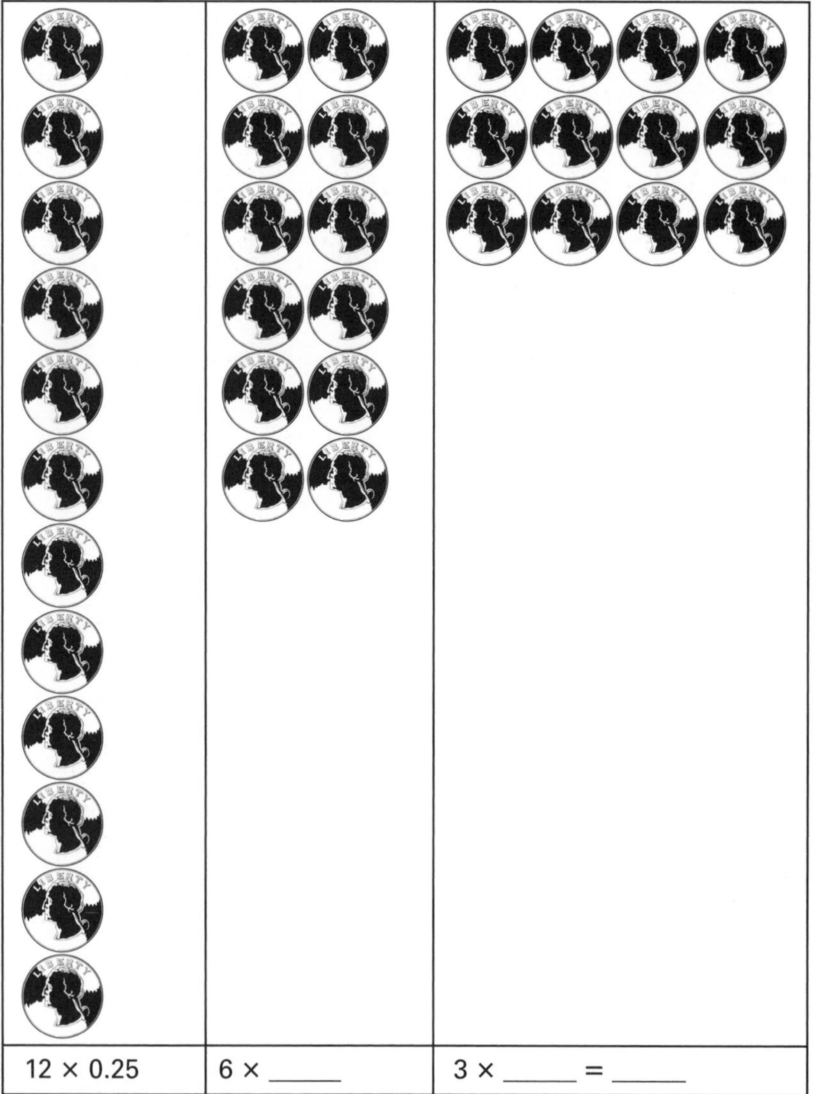

12 × 0.25	6 × _____	3 × _____ = _____

1. Fill in the blanks of the bottom row, to reflect each arrangement. Use the picture to explain this strategy.

2. Use a similar strategy to calculate the following problems mentally. Show your thinking.

a. 8 × $0.25

b. 12 × $0.75

c. 22 × $1.5

d. 16 × $1.25

Name ______________________ Date ____________ Class ____________

Lumber

Chucky's Lumber sells five different lengths of wood; 120 cm, 160 cm, 200 cm, 240 cm, and 280 cm.

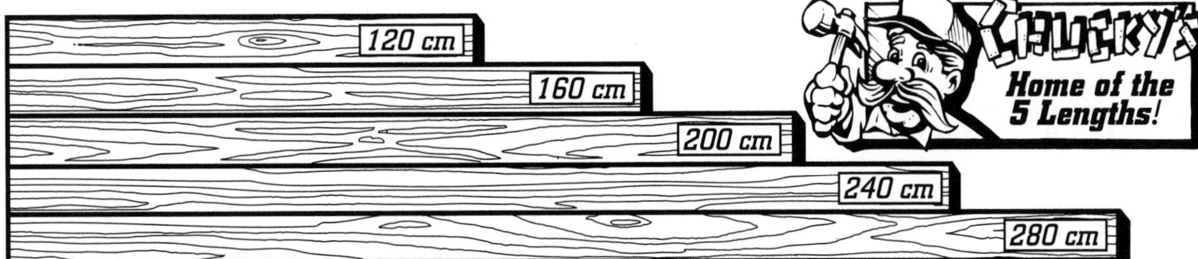

Here are some projects. Find the shortest piece of wood each person needs. Write your answers in the table.

1. Peter is making a bookcase; he needs eight pieces of wood, each 34 cm long.
2. Teresa needs five pieces of wood, each 39 cm long.
3. Hua needs four pieces of wood, each 68 cm long.
4. Bobby needs three pieces of wood, each 82 cm long.
5. Mika needs six pieces of wood, each 41 cm long.
6. Avi needs four pieces of wood, each 63 cm long.
7. Margaret needs six pieces of wood, each 38 cm long.
8. Dieter needs five pieces of wood, each 47 cm long.
9. Uma needs 12 pieces of wood, each 21 cm long.
10. Jennifer needs nine pieces of wood, each 28 cm long.

	Lumber Sizes (in cm)				
	120	160	200	240	280
1.					
2.					
3.					
4.					
5.					
6.					
7.					
8.					
9.					
10.					

Name ______________________ Date ____________ Class ____________

Estimations

Solve these problems without the use of a calculator.

1. Jacqueline earns $4.75 each time she washes her mother's car. How many times does she have to wash the car to save enough money to buy an MP3 player priced at $49?

2. On a shopping trip for his parents, Darnell purchased items worth $4.32, $3.76, $2.58, and $3.84. Estimate the total cost of the four items.

3. A can of baked beans costs $1.49. How many cans could you purchase with $10?

4. At a supermarket checkout, a woman has three items in her cart worth $3.75, $6.92, and $3.83. She realizes that she has only one $10 bill and one $5 bill. Does she have enough money to pay for the items?

5. Dieter needs pieces of lumber in the following lengths:
   2 × 49 cm; 5 × 38 cm; 3 × 21 cm; 1 × 35 cm.

   The lumber is sold in 1-meter lengths. How many 1-meter lengths will Dieter purchase?

6. Natasha works at a computer help desk. She makes notes of the time she spends with each customer.

   A: 14 minutes
   B: 7 minutes
   C: 25 minutes
   D: 12 minutes
   E: 38 minutes
   F: 4 minutes
   G: 12 minutes

   Approximately, how many hours did Natasha spend helping customers?

Name ______________________ Date ____________ Class ____________

Decimal Point (page 1)

1. A school needs to purchase 513 new computers. If each computer costs $3,470, what is the total cost of these new computers? Use your calculator to solve this problem.

DO NOT use your calculator to solve the following problems. Instead, use your answer from problem 1 as a starting point to calculate the new results.

2. A ticket to the circus costs $5.13. If 347 people attended the circus, what is the total ticket revenue?

3. Every year, a ferryboat sails 3,470 times from the mainland to the island of Olku. The maximum number of passengers allowed on the ferry is 5,130. What is the maximum number of people that the boat can carry to the island each year?

4. Pierre pays $34.70 for one kilogram of specialty mushrooms. What would he pay for 5.13 kilograms of mushrooms?

5. Mr. Flores is making some of the costumes for the school play. He needs 51.3 yards of fabric, and the fabric costs $3.47 a yard. What is the total cost for the fabric?

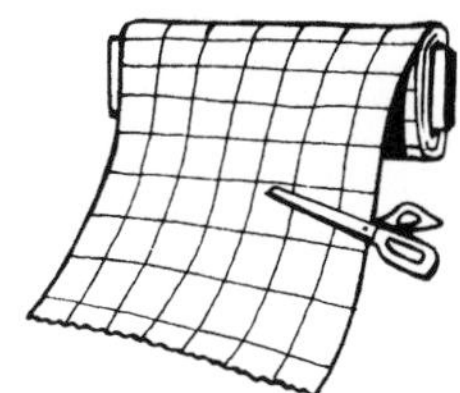

Name ______________________ Date ____________ Class ____________

Decimal Point (page 2)

Louis used a calculator for his homework. Three minutes before handing in his work the next day, he notices that none of his answers has a decimal point. It is too late to re-do the work, so he decides to do each problem mentally. Do you think he can do this in two minutes?

How long does it take you? Time yourself and see how many you complete.

1. a. $6.25 \times 1.3 = 8125$

b. $25.1 \times 4.17 = 104667$

c. $2.125 \times 421.6 = 8959$

d. $0.85 \times 1.5 = 1275$

2. a. $384.75 \div 135 = 285$

b. $384.75 \div 13.5 = 285$

c. $384.75 \div 1.35 = 285$

d. $269.61 \div 28.5 = 946$

5^2 is a shorter notation for 5×5.

Somebody wrote this (we are not telling who!):

$13^2 = 13 \times 13$
$= 109$

$24^2 = 24 \times 24$
$= 416$

1. Use your calculator to show that the two answers are wrong. What did this student do?

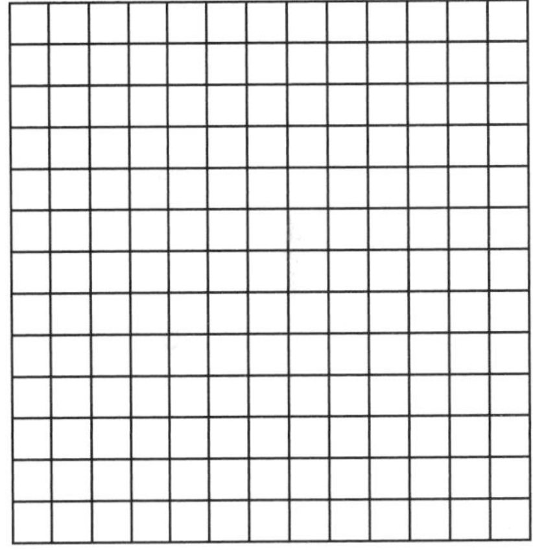

This large square consists of 13 small squares across by 13 small squares down.

2. a. Shade the parts of the large square that represent 10×10 and 3×3.

b. If you think $13^2 = (10 \times 10) + (3 \times 3)$, you are really missing two parts. Write the number of small squares in those two parts.

c. Add the numbers of small squares in the four parts. Is this equal to 13^2?

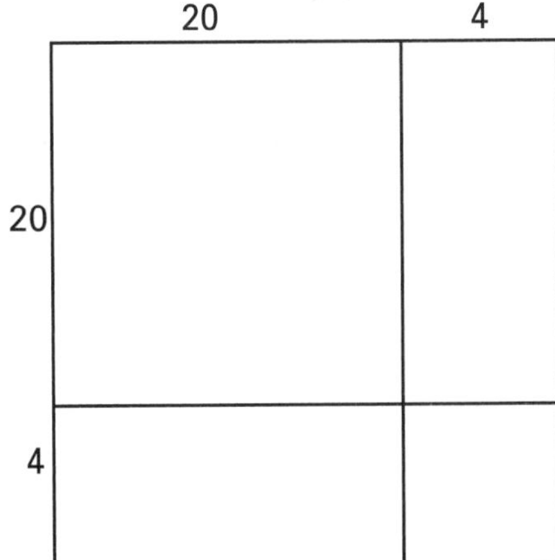

To find 24^2, you can think of a large square that consists of 24 times 24 small squares. You do not have to draw the small squares. You can imagine that they are there and write the dimensions of the four parts along outer edge. The drawing does not need to be to scale.

3. a. Write the number of small squares that would be in each of the four parts if they were all drawn.

b. What is the answer to 24^2 =______?

Name ____________ Date ________ Class ________

Squares (page 2)

3. a. Find the area of each of the four parts.
   b. What is the answer to 15^2?

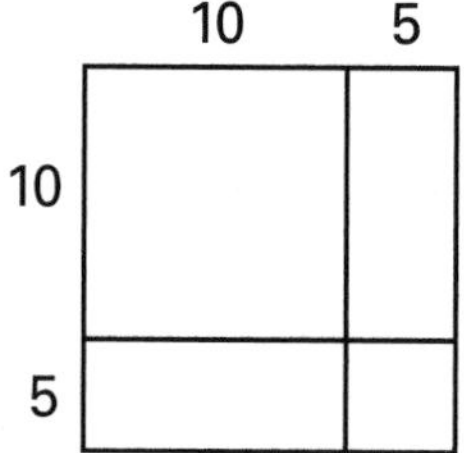

4. a. Find the area of each of the four parts.
   b. What is the answer to 25^2?

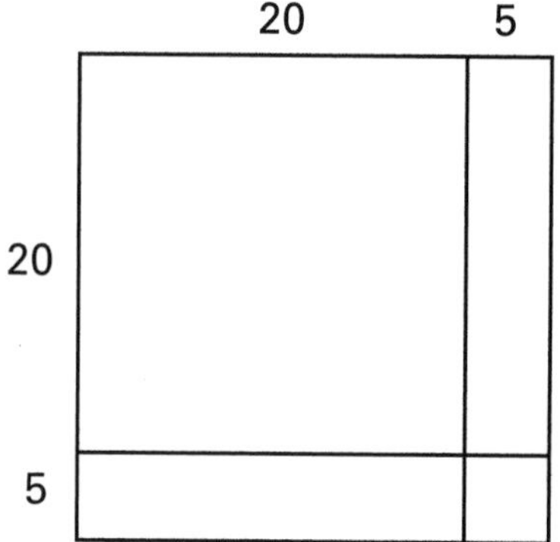

5. Find the answer to 35^2.

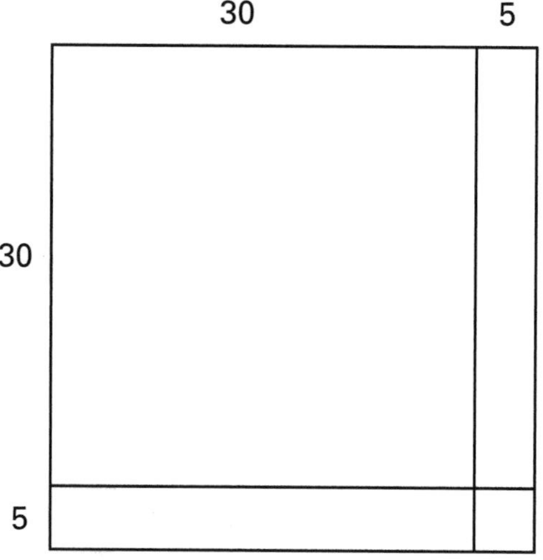

6. Find the answer to 45^2.

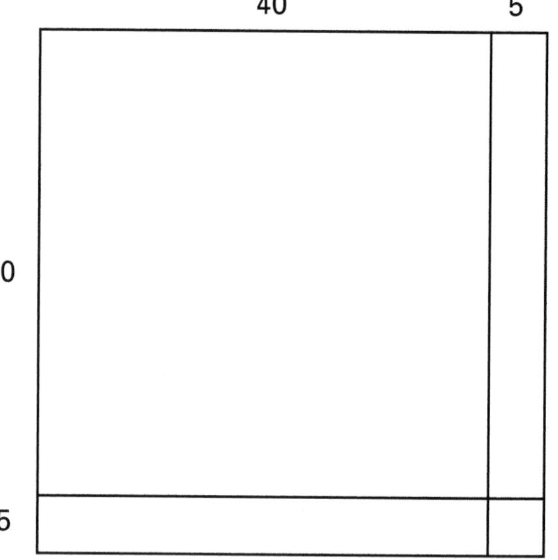

7. Find 55^2 and 65^2.

8. What pattern do you notice? How would you use this pattern to calculate 95^2?

Name ______________________ Date ____________ Class ____________

Rectangles

1. What multiplication problem does this rectangle represent? Perform the calculation.

10 × 20	10 × 7
5 × 20	5 × 7

This rectangle is divided into four parts.

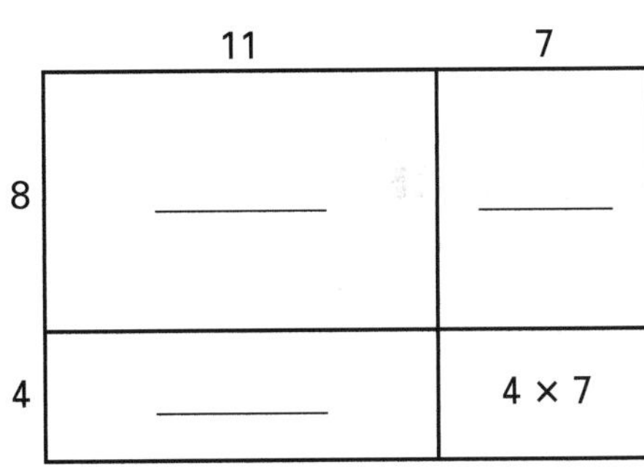

2. a. Fill in the missing numbers in each part.

b. Finish this number sentence showing the computation.

(8 + 4) × (11 + 7)

= 8 × 11 + 8 × 7 + ___ × ___ + ___ × ___

=

=

c. Consider the number sentence showing this computation (10 + 2) × (10 + 8). How do you know, without computing, the answer is the same as in problem 2b?

3. Re-divide the rectangle in problem 2 so that you end up with the same answer, but use different numbers. Write the number sentence showing the computation.

Name ______________________ Date ____________ Class ____________

Different Ways

Abraham and Beth mentally add 235 and 48; without using a calculator or a pencil and paper. Here is what they thought.

235 + 40 is 275:
275 + 8 is 283.
235 + 50 is 285.
It is too much. So
I must subtract 2.
285 – 2 is 283.

This arrow string shows Abraham's mental calculation.

$235 \xrightarrow{+40} 275 \xrightarrow{+8} 283$

1. Write an arrow string showing Beth's mental calculation.

2. Write two different arrow strings that you could use to mentally calculate 492 + 39.

3. Write two different arrow strings that you could use to mentally calculate each of the following problems. Be sure to include your answers.

a. 468 + 29 =		
b. 986 – 91 =		
c. 99 + 250 =		
d. 986 – 49 =		
e. 328 + 28 =		
f. 506 + 58 =		
g. 880 – 28 =		
h. 640 – 48 =		
i. 543 + 39 =		

Name ______________________ Date ____________ Class ____________

very day after school, Jesse plays marbles. Yesterday he started the day with 132 marbles and won 16 more. Today he lost nine marbles.

Each arrow string below shows a method for calculating the number of marbles that Jesse has now.

$132 \xrightarrow{+16} 148 \xrightarrow{-9} 139$

$132 \xrightarrow{+10} 142 \xrightarrow{+6} 148 \xrightarrow{-10} 138 \xrightarrow{+1} 139$

$132 \xrightarrow{+7} 139$

1. Explain why these three arrow strings show the number of marbles that Jesse has now.

Sometimes you can rewrite an arrow string to make the calculation easier. The new arrow string can be shorter or longer than the original but should yield the same result.

2. Here are some other marble results. Make a new arrow string so that it is easy to calculate the number of marbles. Complete the arrow string you created. Try to make some strings longer and others shorter (using only one arrow).

a. $35 \xrightarrow{+1,000}$ ___ $\xrightarrow{-800}$ ___

b. $800 \xrightarrow{+98}$ ___ $\xrightarrow{+100}$ ___

c. $589 \xrightarrow{-100}$ ___ $\xrightarrow{+199}$ ___

d. $763 \xrightarrow{-98}$ ___ $\xrightarrow{-2}$ ___

e. $763 \xrightarrow{-98}$ ___ $\xrightarrow{+2}$ ___

f. $549 \xrightarrow{+31}$ ___ $\xrightarrow{-15}$ ___

g. $800 \xrightarrow{-100}$ ___ $\xrightarrow{+98}$ ___

h. $800 \xrightarrow{+98}$ ___ $\xrightarrow{-100}$ ___

3. You may have written the same arrow string for problems **2g** and **2h**. Why are these strings essentially the same?

Sheila made this longer string for a subtraction problem.

$637 \xrightarrow{-100} 537 \xrightarrow{+3} 540 \xrightarrow{+2} 542$

4. What was her subtraction problem? 637 – ____ = 542

Name ______________________ Date ____________ Class ____________

Multiplication and Division

Mr. Starks has an aquarium in his classroom. In order to find its volume, Mr. Starks's students first determine the aquarium's dimensions, as shown. Maya, Luisa, and Thomas each propose a different arrow string to find the aquarium's volume.

$60 \xrightarrow{\times 40} 2{,}400 \xrightarrow{\times 50} 120{,}000 \text{ cm}^3$

$60 \xrightarrow{\times 50} 3{,}000 \xrightarrow{\times 40} 120{,}000 \text{ cm}^3$

$60 \xrightarrow{\times 2{,}000} 120{,}000 \text{ cm}^3$

1. Compare the three arrow strings. How are the strategies the same? How are they different?

2. For each of the following arrow strings fill in the missing numbers. Then write another arrow string that shows an alternative way to calculate the answer.

a. $8 \xrightarrow{\times 5}$ ____ $\xrightarrow{\times 4}$ ____

b. $32 \xrightarrow{\times 2}$ ____ $\xrightarrow{\times 5}$ ____

c. $50 \xrightarrow{\times 5}$ ____ $\xrightarrow{\div 4}$ ____

d. $750 \xrightarrow{\div 3}$ ____ $\xrightarrow{\times 2}$ ____

e. $1{,}050 \xrightarrow{\div 5}$ ____ $\xrightarrow{\div 2}$ ____

f. $9 \xrightarrow{\times 30}$ ____ $\xrightarrow{\div 30}$ ____

g. $123 \xrightarrow{\times 100}$ ____ $\xrightarrow{\times 5}$ ____

3. Compare the following two arrow strings. Why are the final results different?

$60 \xrightarrow{\times 5}$ ____ $\xrightarrow{+ 40}$ ____ $60 \xrightarrow{+ 40}$ ____ $\xrightarrow{\times 5}$ ____

Name ______________________ Date ____________ Class ____________

Going Backwards

1. Find the result of each of the following arrow strings.

a. 38 $\xrightarrow{+2}$ ___ $\xrightarrow{\times 4}$ ___ $\xrightarrow{-20}$ ___ $\xrightarrow{\div 2}$ ___

b. 70 $\xrightarrow{+50}$ ___ $\xrightarrow{-60}$ ___ $\xrightarrow{\times 3}$ ___ $\xrightarrow{-10}$ ___

c. 5 $\xrightarrow{\times 20}$ ___ $\xrightarrow{-20}$ ___ $\xrightarrow{\times 2}$ ___ $\xrightarrow{\div 2}$ ___

d. 606 $\xrightarrow{+14}$ ___ $\xrightarrow{\times 2}$ ___ $\xrightarrow{-100}$ ___ $\xrightarrow{+50}$ ___

e. 1,000 $\xrightarrow{\div 4}$ ___ $\xrightarrow{\times 4}$ ___ $\xrightarrow{-500}$ ___ $\xrightarrow{+500}$ ___

2. In each of the following arrow strings, the result is given. Fill in all of the missing numbers, especially the first number for each string.

a. ___ $\xrightarrow{\times 2}$ ___ $\xrightarrow{\div 4}$ ___ $\xrightarrow{-20}$ ___ $\xrightarrow{\times 7}$ 35

b. ___ $\xrightarrow{+19}$ ___ $\xrightarrow{\times 2}$ ___ $\xrightarrow{-100}$ ___ $\xrightarrow{-95}$ 5

c. ___ $\xrightarrow{+2}$ ___ $\xrightarrow{\times 2}$ ___ $\xrightarrow{-20}$ ___ $\xrightarrow{\div 2}$ 40

d. ___ $\xrightarrow{+50}$ ___ $\xrightarrow{-10}$ ___ $\xrightarrow{\div 3}$ ___ $\xrightarrow{-2}$ 78

e. ___ $\xrightarrow{+50}$ ___ $\xrightarrow{\div 2}$ ___ $\xrightarrow{-396}$ ___ $\xrightarrow{\times 4}$ 16

3. Make up your own arrow strings with the following results and number of arrows.

a. ___ $\longrightarrow$ ___ $\longrightarrow$ ___ $\longrightarrow$ ___ $\longrightarrow$ 16

b. ___ $\longrightarrow$ ___ $\longrightarrow$ ___ $\longrightarrow$ ___ $\longrightarrow$ 20

c. ___ $\longrightarrow$ ___ $\longrightarrow$ ___ $\longrightarrow$ ___ $\longrightarrow$ 52

4. Make up two arrow strings using other numbers, such as decimals or fraction or integer numbers.

Name ____________________ Date __________ Class __________

Decimals, Fractions, and Division

1. Eight Chess Club members purchased a new chess set for $6. How much was each member's share if everyone contributed the same amount? Explain how you solved this problem.

2. Six musicians play together on the street corner. Today they earn a total of $4 and decide to share the money equally. Joan and Juan want to find each musician's share. Here is how they each solve this problem.

Would you have solved this problem the way Joan did, the way Juan did, or in another way? Why?

3. Complete the table. You can use your calculator. Make up your own problem for the last row.

Division	Fraction	Decimal	Percent
5 ÷ 10			
		0.75	
			10%
2 ÷ 16			
	$\frac{1}{3}$		
			20%
		0.8	
	$\frac{3}{5}$		
15 ÷ 10			

Name ______________________ Date ______________ Class ____________

Cleaning Up

Groups of students from Parker School help clean up the city parks. They earn money by recycling glass bottles and aluminum cans. Each different group shares the money equally.

1. How much money will each student earn in these situations? Write your answers in two ways: as a fraction of a dollar and as dollar amounts. Do not use your calculator.

	Fraction of a Dollar	Money Earned
a. $4 earned by five students		
b. $5 earned by four students		
c. $3 earned by four students		
d. $3 earned by eight students		
e. $6 earned by four students		
f. $6 earned by eight students		

2. If five people earn one dollar, each person gets $\frac{1}{5}$ of a dollar, or 20 cents. You can write this dollar amount as $0.20. If five people earn three dollars, then each person gets $\frac{1}{5}$ of three dollars. How much money is $\frac{1}{5}$ of three dollars? Write one share as a fraction of one dollar.

3. Use your calculator to write each of the following amounts of money.

a. $\frac{1}{8}$ of a dollar
b. $\frac{1}{3}$ of a dollar
c. $\frac{1}{4}$ of a dollar
d. $\frac{3}{5}$ of a dollar
e. $\frac{2}{3}$ of a dollar
f. $3\frac{3}{4}$ dollars
g. $2\frac{5}{6}$ dollars
h. $1\frac{5}{8}$ dollars
i. $9\frac{4}{5}$ dollars
j. $12\frac{3}{20}$ dollars

4. Without using your calculator, name the fraction for each decimal number. When you are finished, use your calculator to check your answers.

a. 0.125
b. 0.25
c. 0.6
d. 0.666666667
e. 0.375
f. 0.75
g. 0.333333333
h. 0.8
i. 0.166666667
j. 0.111111111

Which problem was the easiest? Which was the most challenging?

Name ______________________ Date ____________ Class ____________

Running for Class President (page 1)

At Cleveland Middle School, four students are running for the office of class president. The election will be held in two weeks, so they surveyed 600 students to determine which candidate is currently leading. The table shows the results of the survey.

Results of Class President Survey of 600 Students	
Candidate	**Number of Votes**
Tom Cooper	99
Liza Varelli	204
José da Gamba	153
Lucia Candelo	73
Undecided	71

1. Here are some statements about the survey results. Explain whether each statement is accurate or not accurate.

   a. About $\frac{1}{6}$ of the students say that they will vote for Tom Cooper.

   b. More than $\frac{1}{3}$ say that they will vote for Liza Varelli.

   c. About $\frac{1}{5}$ say that they will vote for José da Gamba.

   d. About $\frac{1}{8}$ say that they will vote for Lucia Candelo.

   e. More than $\frac{1}{6}$ say that they do not know how they will vote.

   f. About 33% of the students say that they will vote for Tom Cooper.

   g. Fewer than 20% say that they will vote for Liza Varelli.

   h. About 40% of the students say that they will vote for José da Gamba.

   i. More than 10% say that they will vote for Lucia Candelo.

   j. More than 20% say that they do not know how they will vote.

Name ____________________ Date ____________ Class ____________

Running for Class President (page 2)

2. Use your calculator to determine the percent of students who will vote for each candidate and the percent of students who are still undecided.

3. Fill in the following pie chart to show the results of the survey. Choose a different color for each candidate and color in the legend and pie chart accordingly.

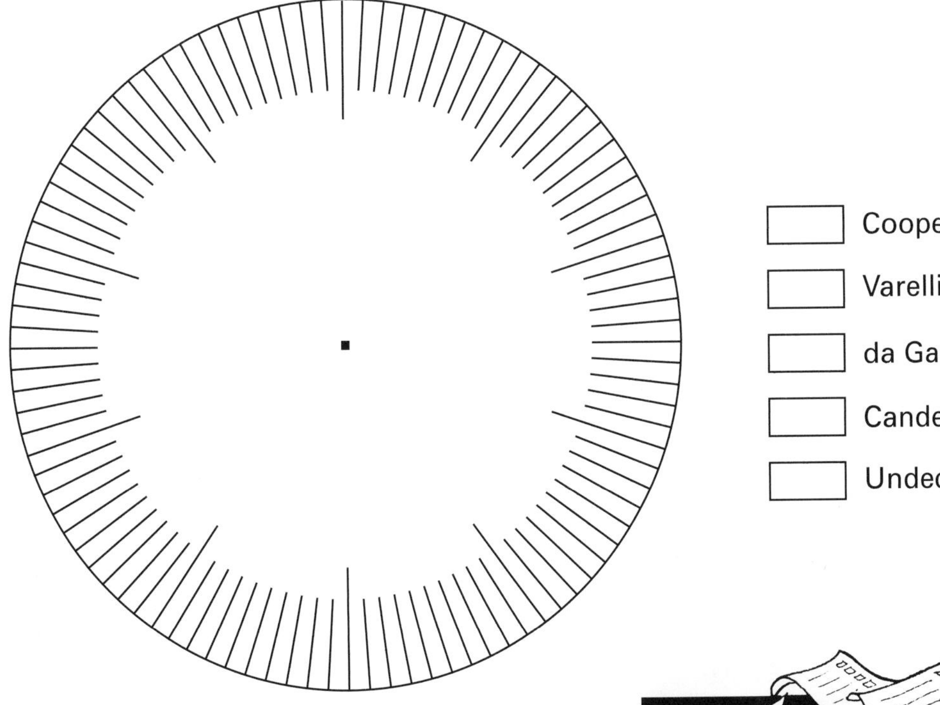

CLASS PRESIDENT
BALLOT BOX

Name ______________________ Date __________ Class __________

Sale

B & B Fashion is having a sale. Stickers indicate the percent discount: 10%, 15%, 20%, 25%, $33\frac{1}{3}$%, or 50%.

The price tag on a sweater is $48, and a sticker shows a discount of 25%. Angela and David each use a different way to calculate the sale price.

A discount of 25% is the same as paying 75%, or $\frac{3}{4}$ of the price. One-fourth of $48.00 is $12.00. 3 × $12.00 = $36.00.
A discount of 25% is the same as $\frac{1}{4}$ off, or $12.00 off. $48.00 – $12.00 = $36.00.

Use either Angela's or David's method to calculate the sale price for each of the following items.

Item	Regular Price	Discount	Sale Price
Jacket	$96.00	25%	
Sweater	$48.00	$33\frac{1}{3}$%	
Jeans	$55.00	10%	
Shoes	$50.00	15%	
Winter Coat	$84.00	50%	
T-Shirt	$ 8.00	20%	
Shorts	$32.00	25%	
Pants	$72.00	$33\frac{1}{3}$%	
Skirt	$82.00	10%	
Dress Shirt	$48.00	25%	

Name ______________________ Date ____________ Class ____________

Which Costs Less?

1. Soft Tunes and Audio Auction feature the same items but offer different discounts. Without using your calculator, circle which store has the lower sale price for each item featured. Be prepared to justify your selection.

Item	Regular Price	Soft Tunes Discount	Audio Auction Discount
CD Player	\$360	25%	\$70 off
Portable Stereo/ CD Player	\$270	$33\frac{1}{3}$%	\$100 off
Speakers	\$548	20%	\$100 off
Stereo Cabinet	\$598	15%	\$100 off

2. Describe two ways to find 20% of \$450.

3. Calculate each of the following.

a. 20% of \$125

b. 25% of \$844

c. $33\frac{1}{3}$% of \$180

d. 10% of \$976

e. 15% of \$620

f. 25% of \$320

g. 10% of \$529

h. $66\frac{2}{3}$% of \$690

i. $33\frac{1}{3}$% of \$219

Name ______________________ Date ____________ Class ____________

On the Number Line

For each number line, find the number indicated by the arrow. For each number line, the hatch marks are the same distance apart.

1.

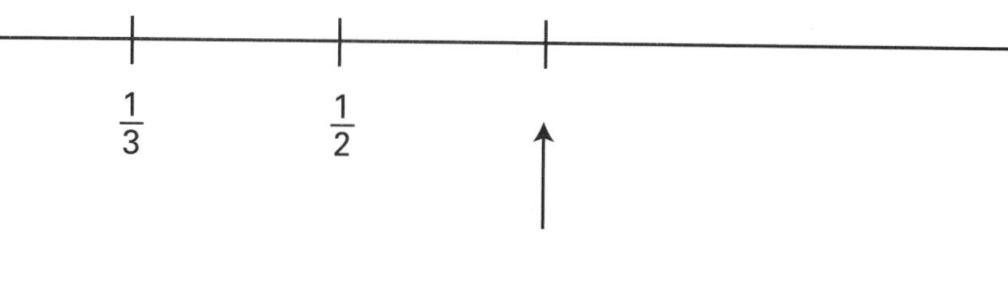

2.

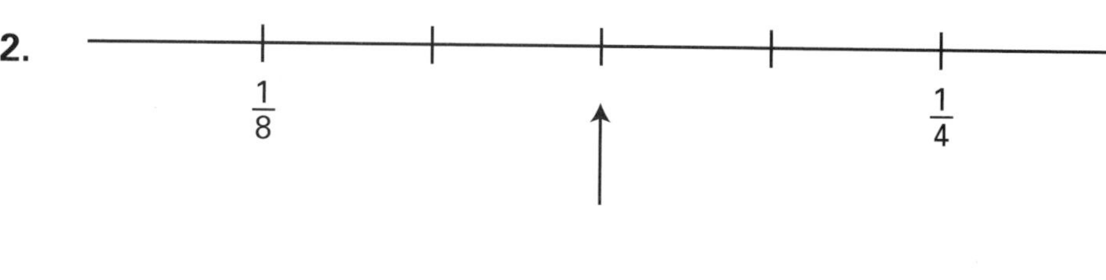

3.

4.

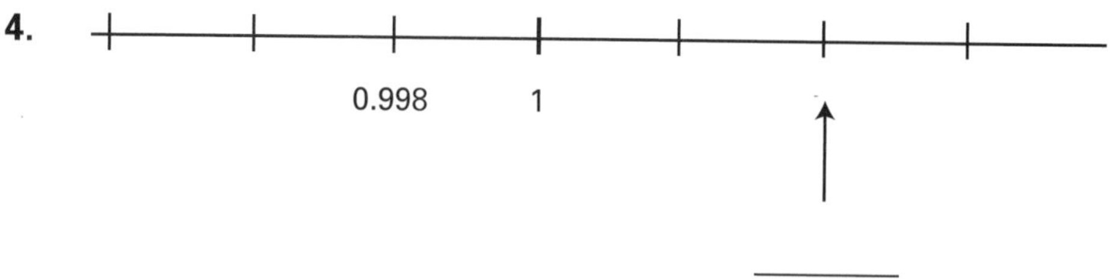

Name ______________________ Date ______________ Class ______________

Comparing Two Schools (page 1)

At Greenfield Middle School, $\frac{2}{3}$ of the students are female. At Brendel Middle School, $\frac{5}{8}$ of the students are female. To determine which school has a larger fraction of female students you can think of two bars with the same number of segments. Here you can use 24 segments.

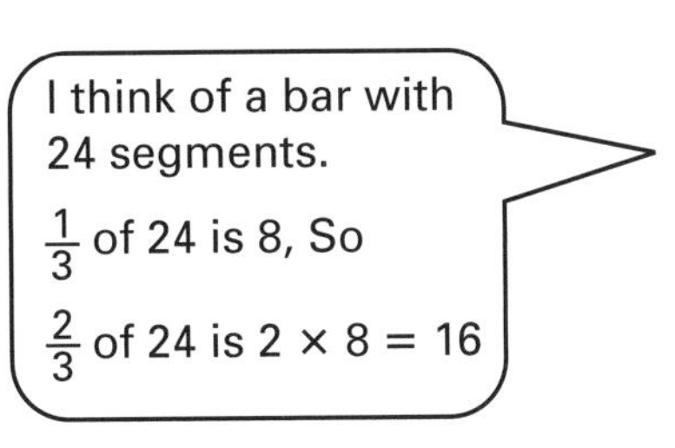

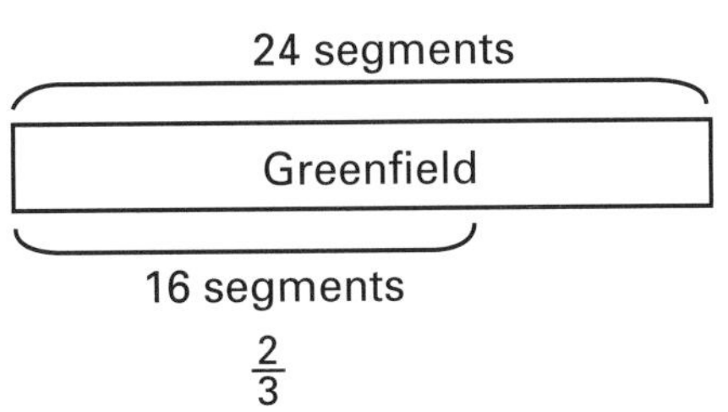

24 segments

Brendel

______ segments

1. a. Complete the bar for Brendel middle school.
   b. Which school has the larger fraction of female students?
   c. Why are 24 segments handy? What other number of segments would have worked too?

2. For each of the following categories, determine which school has the larger fraction of students.

   a. Students Transported by Bus

   Greenfield, $\frac{5}{6}$ of the students

   Brendel, $\frac{3}{4}$ of the students

   b. Seventh-Grade Students

   Greenfield, $\frac{1}{4}$ of the students

   Brendel, $\frac{2}{5}$ of the students

Name ______________________ Date ____________ Class ____________

Comparing Two Schools (page 2)

Gina uses a ratio table to compare fractions. Here is her work for comparing $\frac{5}{6}$ and $\frac{3}{4}$.

$\frac{5}{6}$:

Part	5	10	
Whole	6	12	

$\frac{3}{4}$:

Part	3	6	9
Whole	4	8	12

3. Compare her ratio table strategy with the segmented bars you used to solve problem 2a on the previous page. What do you notice?

4. Compare the following pairs of fractions and circle the larger fraction. You may choose any strategy you like. Show your work or reasoning.

a. $\frac{1}{4}$ and $\frac{1}{5}$

b. $\frac{2}{3}$ and $\frac{5}{8}$

c. $\frac{2}{3}$ and $\frac{4}{9}$

d. $\frac{1}{3}$ and $\frac{2}{5}$

e. $\frac{2}{3}$ and $\frac{1}{2}$

f. $\frac{3}{8}$ and $\frac{1}{4}$

g. $\frac{3}{4}$ and $\frac{4}{5}$

h. $\frac{3}{5}$ and $\frac{3}{4}$

i. $\frac{4}{9}$ and $\frac{1}{3}$

Name ______________________ Date ______________ Class ____________

What Difference?

Among Ms. Washington's students, $\frac{2}{3}$ of the class participates in a sport. Of those students, one-fourth of them play basketball. What fraction of Ms. Washington's class participates in a sport other than basketball? Here is how Thomas solved this problem.

> I think of a class with 24 students. Then $\frac{2}{3}$ of 24 is 16, so 16 students play sports.
> And $\frac{1}{4}$ of 16 is 4, so 4 play basketball.
> That means that 12 play another sport, and 12 out of 24 is the same as $\frac{1}{2}$, so the answer is $\frac{1}{2}$.

1. Among Mr. Guiford's students, $\frac{3}{4}$ of the class participates in a sport. If $\frac{1}{3}$ of the class plays basketball, what fraction of the class participates in a sport other than basketball?
2. At Jefferson Middle School, $\frac{1}{3}$ of the students study a foreign language. If $\frac{2}{9}$ of the students study Japanese, what fraction of the students studies a foreign language other than Japanese?

3. Solve the following subtraction problems.

a. $\frac{3}{8} - \frac{1}{4} =$

b. $\frac{5}{8} - \frac{2}{4} =$

c. $\frac{1}{4} - \frac{1}{6} =$

d. $\frac{4}{5} - \frac{2}{3} =$

e. $\frac{2}{3} - \frac{2}{5} =$

f. $\frac{6}{8} - \frac{2}{3} =$

g. $\frac{2}{3} - \frac{1}{2} =$

h. $\frac{4}{8} - \frac{3}{9} =$

i. $\frac{4}{9} - \frac{2}{6} =$

Name ______________________ Date ____________ Class ____________

Many Zeros

Words	Numeral
One Thousand	1,000
One Million	1,000,000
One Billion	1,000,000,000
One Trillion	1,000,000,000,000

1. Write the following numbers as a numeral using digits.

a. thirteen million ______________________

b. 2 billion ______________________

c. one and a half million ______________________

d. 1.4 million ______________________

e. 2.3 billion ______________________

2. And now the other way around, write each number in words.

a. 7,000,000 ______________________

b. 9,000,000,000 ______________________

c. 15,000,000 ______________________

d. 1,500,000 ______________________

e. 5,000,000,000 ______________________

f. 500,000 ______________________

3. Make up a similar writing exercise. Exchange with a classmate and do each other's problems.

Name ______________________ Date ____________ Class ____________

Here are some population data.

1. Next to each label, write the population as numeral using digits.

Source: http://www.census.gov

120,000,000
115,000,000
110,000,000
105,000,000
100,000,000
95,000,000
90,000,000
85,000,000
80,000,000
75,000,000
70,000,000
65,000,000
60,000,000
55,000,000
50,000,000
45,000,000
40,000,000
35,000,000
30,000,000
25,000,000
20,000,000
15,000,000
10,000,000
5,000,000
0

2. Connect each label to the correct place on the number line. For two labels, this will not be possible; the number line is not long enough.
3. On top of this page, paste a blank sheet of paper. Then extend the number line so that you can connect the label of the United States.
4. Look now at the label of the WORLD. How many extra sheets of paper do you need to connect this label? Explain your answer.

Years, Days, Hours, Seconds

Suppose it is your birthday. People will probably ask how old you are, and your answer will be a certain number of years. How would you answer in terms of days, hours, and/or seconds? Use a calculator to answer the following problems. If the calculator's display is too small for all of the digits, devise another way to answer the problems.

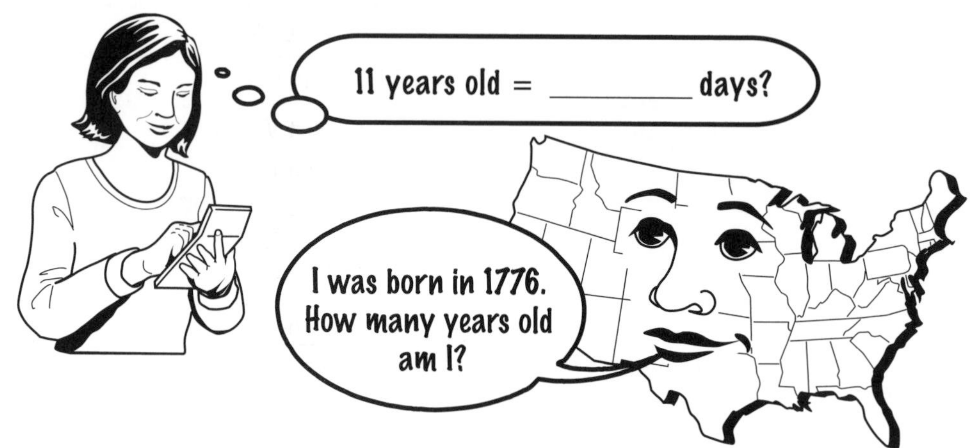

11 years old = ________ days?
I was born in 1776. How many years old am I?

1. How old will you be in years on your next birthday?

2. How old will you be in days on your next birthday?

3. How old will you be in hours on your next birthday?

4. How many years old will the United States be on its next Independence Day? (Hint: The United States became independent in 1776.)

5. How many hours old will the United States be on its next Independence Day?

I can count to one million!
OK, I wanna hear that!

6. How long would this take? Explain your answer, or show your work.

7. How many seconds old will you be on your 60th birthday?

Name ______________________ Date ____________ Class ____________

Rounding (page 1)

Here is data on passenger traffic from some of the world's airports. The data is ordered alphabetically.

1. a. Make a top ten list, ordered by number of passengers.

b. For each city on this top ten list, round the number of passengers to a whole number of millions.

City (Airport)		Total Passengers
1	Atlanta (ATL)	79,086,792
2	Amsterdam (AMS)	39,960,400
3	Bangkok (BKK)	30,175,379
4	Chicago (ORD)	69,508,672
5	Dallas/Fort Worth (DFW)	53,253,607
6	Denver (DEN)	37,505,138
7	Detroit (DTW)	32,664,620
8	Frankfurt/Main (FRA)	48,351,664
9	Hong Kong (HKG)	27,092,290
10	Houston (IAH)	34,154,574
11	Las Vegas (LAS)	36,285,932
12	London (LGW)	30,007,021
13	London/Heathrow (LHR)	63,487,136
14	Los Angeles (LAX)	54,982 838
15	Madrid (MAD)	35,854,293
16	Miami (MIA)	29,595,618
17	Minneapolis/St. Paul (MSP)	33 201,860
18	New York (JFK)	31,732,371
19	Newark (EWR)	29,431,061
20	Orlando (MCO)	27 319,223
21	Paris (CDG)	48,220,436
22	Philadelphia (PHL)	24,671,075
23	Phoenix (PHX)	37,412,165
24	Rome (FCO)	26,284,478
25	San Francisco (SFO)	29,313,271
26	Seattle (SEA)	26 755,888
27	Sydney (SYD)	25,333,508
28	Tokyo (HND)	62,876,269
29	Tokyo (NRT)	26,537,406
30	Toronto (YYZ)	24,739,312

http://www.airports.org

Name ______________________ Date __________ Class __________

Rounding (page 2)

Denver (DEN) had 37,505,138 passengers. You can round this number using a unit of millions: 37,505,138 is about 37.5 million, rounded to the nearest tenth of a million.

2. PHOENIX (PHX) had 37,412,165 passengers. How many million is this? Round this number to the nearest tenth of a million, (one decimal).

3. Which of the following numbers would round to 37.5 million? Explain your answer.

a. 37,505,876

b. 37,598,652

c. 37,389,989

d. 37,456,789

4. Find the lowest and the highest number of passengers that would round to 37.5 million.

5. Round the following prices to cents.

a. $11.435

b. $326.6249

c. $2865.996

d. $21.445

Naomi bought a T-shirt. When her mother asked her what she paid for it, she answered, "Oh, about 20 dollars."

6. a. Name one possible price of Naomi's T-shirt.

b. Name the lowest and the highest possible price for Naomi's T-shirt. You may assume that Naomi rounded the price to a whole number of dollars.

Name ______________________ Date ____________ Class ____________

Track Your Time and Accuracy (page 1)

Do each problem as quickly as you can.

Record your Start Time:

1. a. $10 \times 28 =$

   b. $5 \times 28 =$

2. a. $2 \times 5 \times 7 =$

   b. $2 \times 18 \times 5 =$

3. a. $10 \times 30 =$

   b. $20 \times 30 =$

4. a. $10 \times 3.1 =$

   b. $100 \times 3.1 =$

5. a. $3 \times 30 =$

   b. $6 \times 15 =$

6. a. $10 \times 15 =$

   b. $11 \times 15 =$

7. a. $10 \times 25 =$

   b. $9 \times 25 =$

8. a. $40 \div 10 =$

   b. $4 \div 10 =$

9. a. $6 \times 15 =$

   b. $8 \times 45 =$

10. a. $1.2 \times$ ____ $= 12$

    b. $1.2 \times$ ____ $= 6$

Record Your Finish Time:

Fill in your results. Keep track of your results. With practice, you will improve both your speed and accuracy.

My Results:

Total Time ____________

Total Correct ____________

Track Your Time and Accuracy (page 2)

Do each problem as quickly as you can.

Record your Start Time: 

1. a. 10 × 23 =
   b. 20 × 23 =

2. a. 4 × 60 =
   b. 8 × 60 =

3. a. 10 × 21 =
   b. 20 × 21 =

4. a. 2 × 5 × 9 =
   b. 2 × 17 × 5 =

5. a. 10 × 5.2 =
   b. 100 × 5.2 =

6. a. 10 × 25 =
   b. 11 × 25 =

7. a. 10 × 15 =
   b. 9 × 15 =

8. a. 60 ÷ 10 =
   b. 6 ÷ 10 =

9. a. 6 × 25 =
   b. 8 × 35 =

10. a. 1.4 × ____ = 14
    b. 1.4 × ____ = 7

Record your Finish Time: [ ]

Fill in your results. Keep track of your results. With practice, you will improve both your speed and accuracy.

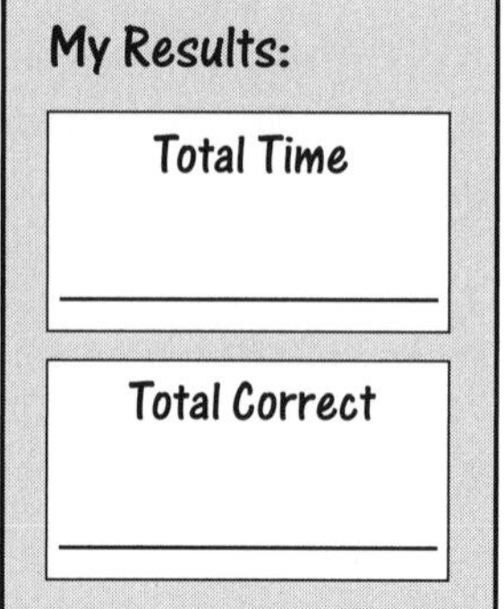

My Results:

Total Time ____________

Total Correct ____________

Name ______________________ Date ____________ Class ____________

1. a. Create ten problems similar to the previous problems. Of course, you have to provide the answers to your problems.
   b. Exchange your problems with a classmate.
   c. Keep a clean copy of your problems so that you can exchange problems with a classmate whenever there is time. Continue to keep a record of your improvements in speed and accuracy. You may want to record your scores in a table and graph the results.

Record your Start Time: ______

Record your Finish Time: ______

My Results:

Total Time ______

Total Correct ______

Name ______________________ Date ____________ Class ____________

Ways to Write Numbers (page 1)

	Numbers						
Arabic Numerals	1	9	10	19	38	93	100
Roman Numerals	I	IX	X	XIX	XXXVIII	XCIII	C
English Words	one	nine	ten	nineteen	thirty-eight	ninety-three	one hundred
French Words	un	neuf	dix	dix-neuf	trente-huit	quatrevingt-treize	cent
Spanish Words	uno	nueve	diez	diecinueve	treinta y ocho	noventa y tres	cien
Portuguese Words	um	nove	dez	dezanove	trinta e oito	noventa e três	cem

1. Use the information in this table to describe similarities and differences in the way numbers are written.

Our Number System is a positional system, which uses the digits 0 through 9. The first base unit is ten. You can compose all of the numbers using a base of ten.

Most of the numbers between ten and twenty have names that reflect the addition operation. *Eleven* and *twelve* are exceptions; these words do not reflect the addition operation.

Name	Composition
thir-teen	3 + 10
four-teen	4 + 10
fif-teen	?

2. How would you compose *for-ty*, and *six-ty*?

To compose numbers larger than nineteen, you need to use a combination of operations. For example, thirty-four is composed of 3 tens and 4 ones: $3 \times 10 + 4$; seven hundred thirty-four is composed of 7 hundreds, 3 tens, and 4 ones: $7 \times 100 + 3 \times 10 + 4$.

3. Write each number word as a numeral and as a composition reflecting the words.

Word Name	Numeral	Composition
a. five hundred sixty-five		
b. two hundred fifty		
c. three thousand five hundred		
d. thirty-five hundred		

Name ______________________ Date______________ Class____________

4. Compare your answers to **c** and **d**. What do you notice?

5. a. What is a different word name for one thousand nine hundred fifty?

b. Write two different number compositions for both word names.

Hank volunteers at the homeless shelter. Hank's job today is to place 350 free meal coupons into envelopes, with 10 coupons in each envelope.

6. a. How many envelopes will Hank fill today?

b. Yesterday, Hank placed 2,351 meal coupons into envelopes. How many envelopes did he fill yesterday?

Hank places the extra coupon(s) in an envelope and marks it "partial."

c. What fractional part of an envelope is this? What decimal part of an envelope is this?

d. What if Hank fills each envelop with 100 coupons? How would your answers for **a**, **b**, and **c** change?

There are many ways to describe the number 2,351.
A common way to describe 2,351 is to expand it:
2 thousands, 3 hundreds, 5 tens, and 1 ones.

Here are some other ways to describe 2,351.

2,351 is 2,351 ones. 2,351 is 23.51 hundreds.
2,351 is 235.1 tens. 2,351 is 2.351 thousands.

thousands	hundreds	tens	ones
2	3	5	1

7. a. Explain these five different ways to describe 2,351.

b. Describe the number 350 in four different ways.

c. Describe the number 15,387 in six different ways.

8. Write one numeral for each number word description.

a. 6 thousands, 9 hundreds, and 5 ones

b. 5.673 thousands

c. 3,478.9 tens

d. 34.76 hundreds

e. 125.5 hundreds

Name ______________________ Date ____________ Class ____________

Powers of Ten (page 1)

Our number system is based on powers of ten. You can use powers of 10 as a shortcut to describe numbers. Recall that 100 is 10×10 or 10^2, read as "ten to the second power," or "ten squared."

For most powers of ten, we have special names, but not for all.

$10^2 = 10 \times 10 = 100$, or one hundred

$10^3 = 10 \times 10 \times 10 = 1{,}000$, or one thousand

The next special name is one million, which is 1,000,000, or 10^6.

1. **a.** In the table on the next page you see the names for large numbers. Write these numbers as powers of ten.

   b. What pattern do the powers of ten have?

You can describe each number in the table that is larger than 1,000 as a power of 1,000. For example, 1,000,000 is $1{,}000 \times 1{,}000$, or $1{,}000^2$.

2. Fill in the last column of the table.

3. Calculate the following products. Write your answers as a power of ten.

   a. $10 \times 1{,}000 =$

   b. $1{,}000 \times 1{,}000 =$

   c. $1{,}000 \times 1{,}000 \times 1{,}000 =$

   d. $100^2 =$

   e. $100^2 \times 100^2 =$

   f. $10^4 \times 10^3 =$

   g. $10^3 \times 10^2 \times 10 =$

4. Calculate the following quotients. Write your answers as a power of ten.

   a. $1{,}000{,}000 \div 1{,}000 =$

   b. $1{,}000{,}000{,}000 \div 1{,}000 =$

   c. $1{,}000 \div 10 =$

   d. $10^6 \div 10 =$

   e. $10^8 \div 10^3 =$

   f. $10^{10} \div 10^5 =$

   g. $10^3 \div 10^3 =$

Name ______________________ Date ____________ Class ____________

Powers of Ten (page 2)

as Numeral	in Words	Power of 10	Power of 1,000
10	ten		
100	hundred		
1,000	thousand		
1,000,000	million		$1,000^2$
1,000,000,000	billion		
1,000,000,000,000	trillion		
	quadrillion		
	quintillion		
	sextillion		
	septillion		
	octillion		
	nonillion		
	decillion		
	undecillion		
	duodecillion		
	tredecillion		
	quattuordecillion		
	quindecillion		
	sexdecillion		
	septendecillion		
	octodecillion		
	novemdecillion		
	vigintillion		
	unvigintillion		
	duovigintillion		
	trevigintillion		
	quattuorvigintillion		
	quinvigintillion		

Name ______________________ Date ____________ Class ____________

More Powers

You can write 2 million as the product of a number and a power of ten: 2×10^6.

1. For the following problems, write your answers as a product of a number and a power of ten.

   a. 2 million + 3 million

   b. 2 billion + 1.5 billion

   c. 7.5 thousand − 3.5 thousand

   d. $2 \times 10^3 + 5 \times 10^3$

   e. $3 \times 10^6 - 1.5 \times 10^6$

   f. 500,000 + 1 million

   g. $20 \times 10^5 + 4 \times 10^6$

Here are four different strategies to add 2 million and 5 thousand.

Ayla

2 million is equal to 2,000 thousand, so
2,000 thousand + 5 thousand =
2,005 thousand or $2{,}005 \times 10^3$

Carlo

$2 \times 10^6 + 5 \times 10^3 =$
$2{,}000 \times 10^3 + 5 \times 10^3 =$
$2{,}005 \times 10^3$

Brad

$2 \times 10^6 + 5 \times 10^3 =$
$2 \times 10^6 + 0.005 \times 10^6 =$
2.005×10^6

Felicia

2,000,000 + 5,000 =
2,005,000 =
2.005×10^6

2. a. Compare these four strategies. How are they different? How are they the same?

   b. Which strategy do you like the most? Why?

3. Write your answers as a product of a number and a power of ten. Use two different strategies.

   a. 5 million + 20 thousand

   b. 7 billion + 400 million

   c. $3 \times 10^3 + 7 \times 10^4$

   d. $5.0 \times 10^7 - 6.5 \times 10^5$

Name ______________________ Date__________ Class__________

Units (page 1)

Here are two different rulers. One is marked with inches and the other with centimeters.

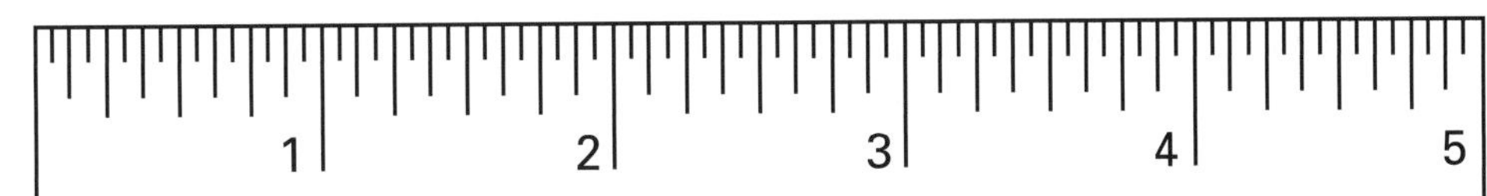

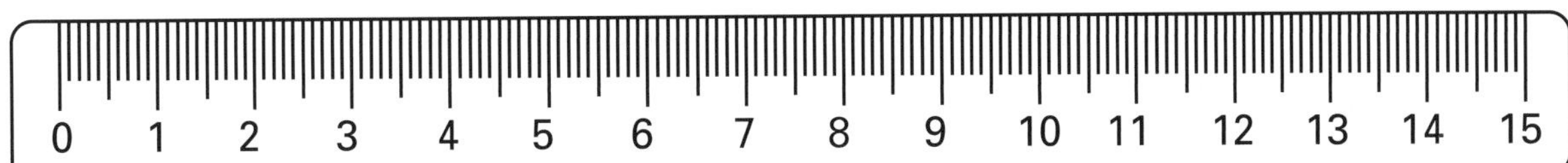

1. a. Which ruler—the first or the second—shows centimeters? How do you know?

b. Both the centimeter and inch are partitioned into smaller units. Compare and contrast these partitions. Which one is based on units of ten?

2. You may use the two rulers to complete:

a. one inch is about __________ centimeters.

b. one centimeter is about _________ inch.

3. How long is one meter? Look around you. Is there anything in the classroom that is about one meter long or wide or high?

4. Compare a meter stick with a yardstick. Which one is based on units of ten?

5. Leo states that a meter is approximately 10% longer than a yard. Is he right? Explain.

A centimeter (cm) is one-hundredth of a meter (m).

There are two different ways to describe this relationship, with a fraction and with a decimal.

$1 \text{ cm} = \frac{1}{100} \text{ m}$ $\quad$ $1 \text{ cm} = 0.01 \text{ m}$

6. Describe each of the following relationships in two ways, with a fraction and with a decimal.

	Fraction	**Decimal**
a.	2 cm = _______ m	2 cm = _______ m
b.	__ cm = $\frac{1}{2}$ m	__ cm = _______ m
c.	25 cm = _______ m	25 cm = _______ m
d.	7.5 cm = _______ m	7.5 cm = _______ m

Name ______________________ Date__________ Class__________

Units (page 2)

The height of this MP3 player is one decimeter.

This height is drawn in its actual size.

7. **a.** How many centimeters is this?

   b. How many decimeters are in one meter?

8. Use two different ways to describe the relationship between a decimeter and a meter, with a fraction and with a decimal.

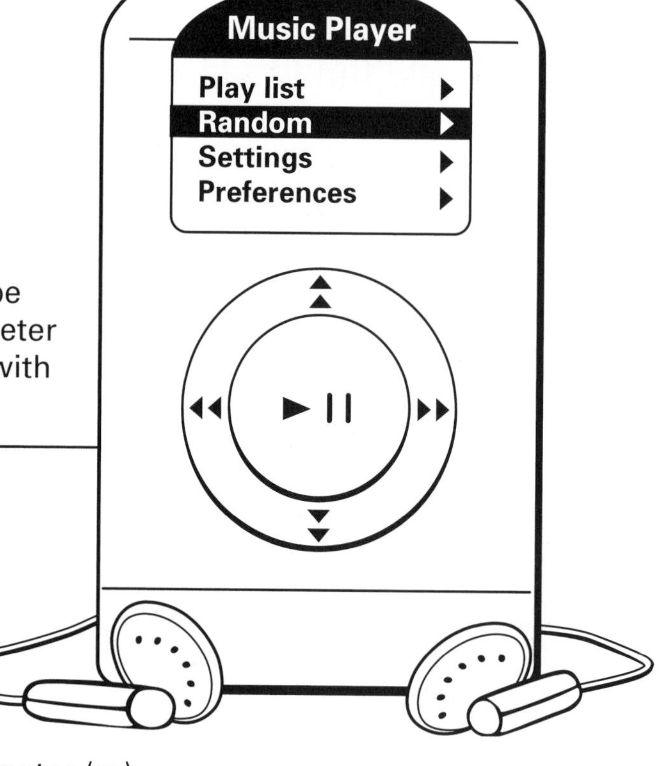

Millimeters, centimeters, decimeters, and **meters** are metric units used to measure length.

The prefixes, *deci*, *centi*, and *milli*, are derived from Latin.

Deci means one-tenth.

One decimeter (dm) is one-tenth of a meter (m).

Centi means one-hundredth.

One centimeter (cm) is one-hundredth of a meter.

Milli means one-thousandth.

One millimeter (mm) is one-thousandth of a meter.

9. Describe each of the following relationships in two ways, with a fraction and with a decimal.

	Fraction	**Decimal**
a.	1 mm = ______ m	1 mm = ______ m
b.	1 mm = ______ cm	1 mm = ______ cm
c.	3 dm = ______ m	3 dm = ______ m
d.	2.5 cm = ______ dm	2.5 cm = ______ dm
e.	7.5 mm = ______ cm	7.5 mm = ______ cm

Name ______________________ Date__________ Class__________

In the United States, most people use the Customary System rather than the metric system. The inch (in.) is a unit for measuring length in the Customary System.

1. What other measurement units for length do you know? And for weight? And volume?

2. Complete these sentences with the appropriate unit.

   a. The width of a door is about 1 ________ .

   b. The height of my bicycle is about 20 ________ .

   c. The length of the hallway is about 30 ________.

   d. The small town is about 2 ________ wide.

Here is a ruler with inches.

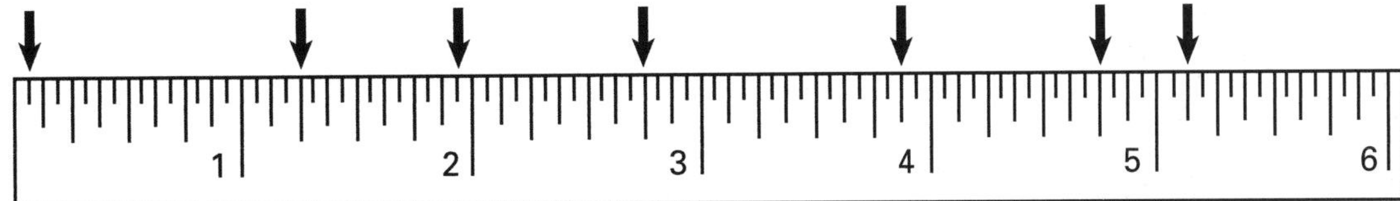

3. a. How do you know that this ruler not based on units of ten?

   b. How is each inch partitioned?

   c. Use a mixed number to write the number of inches indicated by each arrow. Use the abbreviation, ″, for inches.

4. Calculate each sum. Remember that 12 in. = 1 ft. The abbreviation, ′, is for feet.

   a. $2\frac{1}{2}'' + 1\frac{1}{4}'' =$

   b. $1\frac{1}{8}'' + \frac{3}{4}'' + 2\frac{1}{2}'' =$

   c. $7'\ 2\frac{3}{4}'' + 11'\ 5\frac{1}{4}'' =$

   d. $12'\ 9'' + 13'\ 2\frac{1}{2}'' + 5'\ 3\frac{3}{4}'' =$

5. Write each length in a different form.

   a. 5 ft 7 in. = ______ in.

   b. 75 in. = ______ ft ______ in.

   c. $3\frac{2}{3}$ yd = ______ ft

   d. $10\frac{1}{3}$ yd = ______ in.

Name ______________________ Date ______________ Class ______________

Metric System (page 1)

There are three base units in the metric system; the meter for length, the gram for weight or mass, and the liter for volume or capacity.

Multiples and fractions of these units are created by adding prefixes to the names of the defined units. For example, the prefix ***kilo*** means one thousand, so 1 ***kilo***meter is 1,000 meters.

		Meaning		
Prefix	**Symbol**	**as a Number**	**as a Power of Ten**	**in Words**
Tera-	T-			Trillion
Giga-	G-			Billion
Mega-	M-			Million
Kilo-	k-			Thousand
Hecto-	h-	100	10^2	Hundred
Deca-	da-	10	10^1	Ten
Base Unit:				**Measures:**
Meter	m	1	10^0	Length
Gram	g	1		Weight
Liter	l	1		Volume
Deci-	d-	0.1	10^{-1}	Tenth
Centi-	c-	0.01		Hundredth
Milli-	m-	0.001		Thousandth
Micro-	μ-			Millionth
Nano-	n-			Billionth
Pico-	p-			Trillionth

1. Write five measurement units that have one of these prefixes and explain how it compares to its basic unit of meter, gram, or liter.

2. Write each prefix as a number by filling in the third column.

3. a. Write each prefix as a power of ten by filling in the fourth column.

b. What pattern do you notice in the fourth column, Meaning as a Power of Ten?

Name ______________________ Date______________ Class______________

4. Fill in the correct prefix, written out fully and abbreviated.

   a. My pencil is about 150 ______ meters (___ m).

   b. The circumference of the earth is about 40,000 ______ meters (___ m).

   c. A hair grows approximately 0.3 ______ meters (___ m) a day.

   d. A door is about 200 ______ meters (___ m).

Five decimeters is five-tenths of a meter. Here are three ways to write this relationship.

5 dm = $\frac{5}{10}$ meter, as a fraction;
5 dm = 0.5 meter, as a decimal; and
5 dm = 5×10^{-1} meter, as a product of a number and a power of 10.

5. Describe each of the following relationships in three ways: as a fraction, as a decimal, and as a product of a number and a power of ten.

	Fraction	Decimal	Product (# × 10)
a. 5 cm			
b. 7 dm			
c. 15 mm			

You can see how small a millimeter is by looking at a centimeter ruler. How small is a micrometer?

6. Do you think you can see something of the size of one micrometer (μm)? Explain why or why not.

The size of a virus is between 0.02 and 0.25 μm.

7. Convert these measures to millimeters.

Nanotechnology is a branch of engineering that develops and uses devices that have sizes of only a few nanometers. Nanotechnology is sometimes called molecular manufacturing.

8. What fraction of a millimeter is one nanometer?

Name ______________________ Date ____________ Class ____________

A Little about Liters

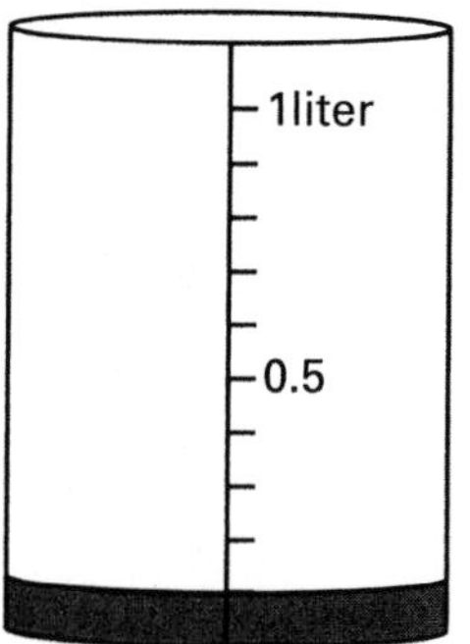

Here is a graduated cylinder. You can measure the volume of a liquid by reading the water level. The markings on the cylinder indicate that you can measure up to one liter of liquid.

1. What is the water level of this cylinder?
   What is the volume of the liquid?

2. What interval markings would you want on the cylinder if you had to measure 0.07 liter of liquid?

Milliliters (ml), centiliters (cl), deciliters (dl), and **liters(l)** are metric units used to measure liquid volume.

milli means one-thousandth	one milliliter = $\frac{1}{1000}$ liter
centi means one-hundredth	one centiliter = $\frac{1}{100}$ liter
deci means one-tenth	one deciliter = $\frac{1}{10}$ liter

3. A tin can holds 0.33 liter of lemonade. Mark the level on this graduated cylinder to show 0.33 liter of lemonade.

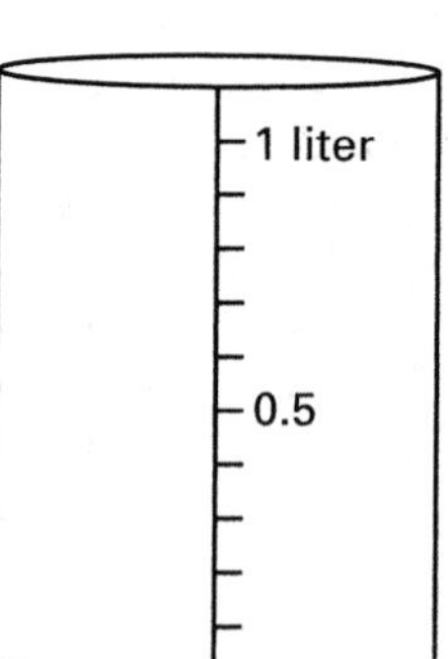

4. **a.** How much is 0.33 liter in deciliters?

   0.33 liter = ____ deciliters

   b. How much is 0.33 liter in centiliters?

   0.33 liter = ____ centiliters

   c. How much is 0.33 liter in milliliters?

   0.33 liter = ____ milliliters

5. **a.** Draw the level of the liquid in each cylinder to show the given amount.

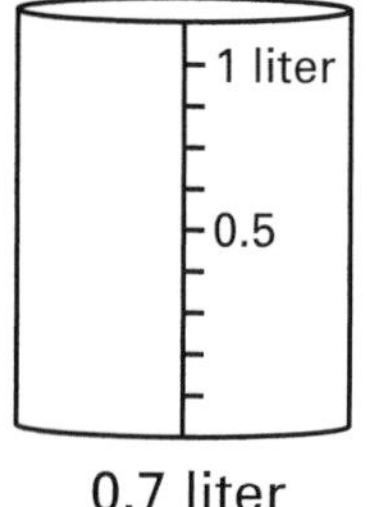

0.7 liter

0.07 liter

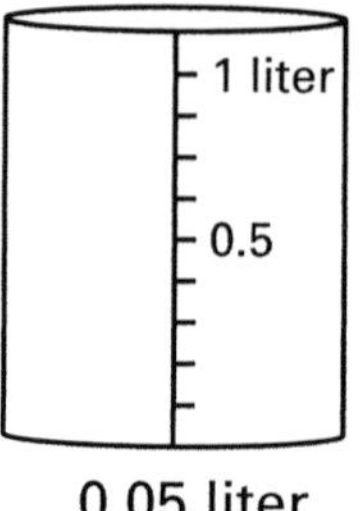

0.05 liter

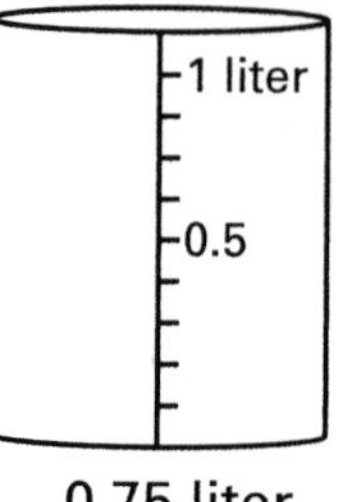

0.75 liter

   b. Order the amounts of liquid shown in part **a** from smallest to largest.

Around 1800, the meter was designed to be one ten-millionth of the distance between the Equator and the North Pole.

1. According to this design, how far is the North Pole from the Equator in meters? And in kilometers?

Several signs in Wisconsin and upper Michigan mark the halfway point between the Equator and the North Pole. There are two different ways to define halfway between the Equator and the North Pole. Here you see an example of each.

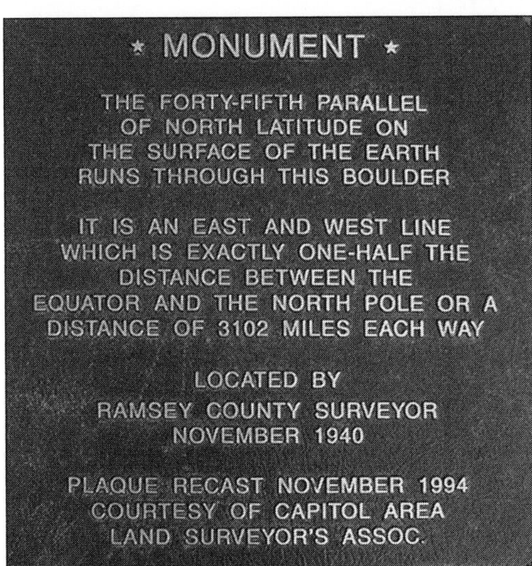

2. a. What are the two different ways to define halfway between the Equator and the North Pole?

   b. Use the information on each sign to calculate the distance, in miles, from the North Pole to the Equator.

You have the distance between the Equator and the North Pole measured with two different units, a meter and a mile.

3. Use your answers to problems 1 and 2 to find two relationships between a meter and a mile.

Today, the meter is defined precisely; one mile is about 1609.344 meters.

4. Today, what is the precise distance from the equator to the North Pole? Calculate the distance in meters and in kilometers.

Name ______________________ Date__________ Class__________

How Fast? (page 1)

1. Marge drove 65 miles from Springfield to Boville. She left Springfield at 2:00 P.M. and arrived in Boville at 3:15 P.M. She uses this ratio table to find the average speed for her trip. Explain Marge's method.

Distance (in mi)	65	260	52
Time (in hours)	$1\frac{1}{4}$	5	1

2. Instead of writing $1\frac{1}{4}$ hours for the travel time, you can use quarters of an hour or minutes. Find the average speed for Marge's trip using the following ratio tables.

Distance (in mi)	65				
Time (in quarter hours)	5				

Distance (in mi)	65				
Time (in minutes)	75				

Name ______________________ Date ____________ Class ____________

How Fast? (page 2)

3. Use a ratio table to calculate the average speed for each of the following trips.

a. Departure Time: 8:00 A.M. Arrival Time: 9:30 A.M.
Distance Traveled: 81 miles

Distance (in mi)					
Time (in)					

b. Departure Time: 2:00 P.M. Arrival Time: 5:30 P.M.
Distance Traveled: 140 miles

Distance (in mi)					
Time (in)					

c. Departure Time: 8:15 A.M. Arrival Time: 10:00 A.M.
Distance Traveled: 84 miles

Distance (in mi)					
Time (in)					

d. Departure Time: 9:05 A.M. Arrival Time: 9:55 A.M.
Distance Traveled: 30 miles

Distance (in mi)					
Time (in)					

e. Departure Time: 7:30 A.M. Arrival Time: 4:00 P.M.
Distance Traveled: 170 miles

Distance (in mi)					
Time (in)					

4. The average speed for the trip in part **e** above is very slow. Provide a possible explanation for the slow average speed.

Name ______________________ Date ____________ Class ____________

Gas Mileage (page 1)

Mr. Van Dyke's science students are calculating the gas mileage of different cars. Gas mileage is the average number of miles that a car can travel on one gallon of gas.

1. Arnold is figuring out the gas mileage for a car that was driven 210 miles on 8.4 gallons of gas. He begins his calculations as shown here.

Distance (in mi)	210	2,100	300			
Gas (in gallons)	8.4	84				

a. Explain Arnold's first step.

b. Explain his next step.

c. Complete Arnold's calculations to find the car's gas mileage.

Name ______________________ Date ____________ Class ____________

Gas Mileage (page 2)

2. Using ratio tables, calculate the gas mileage for each of the following.

a. A car travels 108 miles on 6 gallons of gasoline.

Distance (in mi)					
Gas (in gallons)					

b. A car travels 252 miles on 12 gallons of gasoline.

Distance (in mi)					
Gas (in gallons)					

c. A car travels 121 miles on 5.5 gallons of gasoline.

Distance (in mi)					
Gas (in gallons)					

d. A car travels 164 miles on 8 gallons of gasoline.

Distance (in mi)					
Gas (in gallons)					

e. A car travels 82.5 miles on 5.5 gallons of gasoline.

Distance (in mi)					
Gas (in gallons)					

3. If a car averages 20.5 miles per gallon of gas, how many gallons are needed to travel 492 miles? Use the following ratio table to calculate your answer.

Distance (in mi)					
Gas (in gallons)					

Name ______________________ Date__________ Class__________

Gas Mileage Again (page 1)

Caroline's car averages 24 miles per gallon, which means that it needs 1 gallon of gas to travel 24 miles. Last year, Caroline drove her car 29,848 miles. She uses the following ratio table to calculate how many gallons of gas she used in her car during the year.

Distance (in mi)	24	24,000	4,800	960	29,760
Gas (in gallons)	1	1,000	200	40	1,240

Caroline concludes that she used a little more than 1,240 gallons of gas last year.

1. a. Explain Caroline's method.

b. Show another way to use a ratio table to calculate the number of gallons of gas Caroline used in her car last year.

Name ______________________ Date______________ Class______________

Gas Mileage Again (page 2)

2. For each of the following car trips, use a ratio table to find the approximate number of gallons of gas used. Then check your work with a calculator.

a. Mr. Sommers drove 195 miles, and his car averages 24 miles per gallon.

Distance (in mi)					
Gas (in gallons)					

b. Ms. Donno drove 316 miles, and her car averages 18 miles per gallon.

Distance (in mi)					
Gas (in gallons)					

c. Ms. Bartok drove 428 miles, and her car averages 23 miles per gallon.

Distance (in mi)					
Gas (in gallons)					

d. Mr. Aspen drove 391 miles, and his car averages 22 miles per gallon.

Distance (in mi)					
Gas (in gallons)					

e. Mr. Yuanes drove his car a total of 19,362 miles last year, and his car averages 21 miles per gallon.

Distance (in mi)					
Gas (in gallons)					

Name ______________________ Date __________ Class __________

Population (page 1)

1. In Sun City, there is one horse for every five people. What is the horse to people ratio for Moon City? You may want to use a ratio table for your calculations.

2. In Dustown, there are 28 horses per 100 inhabitants.

   a. Which town has the least number of horses relative to its population—Sun City, Moon City, or Dustown?

   b. The population of Dustown is 1,368. How many horses are there in the town?

Population (page 2)

3. Summarize the following information as a ratio (_____ per 100).

   a. Switzerland has approximately 7,404,055 inhabitants and 3,940,000 television sets.

   b. Taiwan has approximately 22,647,000 inhabitants and 13,355,000 telephones.

   c. Greece has approximately 11,000,000 inhabitants and 5,220,000 radios.

   d. Japan has approximately 127.5 million inhabitants. Each day, approximately 73,300,000 newspapers are sold.

   e. Jamaica has approximately 2,644,000 inhabitants and 168,179 passenger cars.

Name ______________________ Date ____________ Class ____________

Car (page 1)

The table shows the number of passenger cars and the population in several countries.

Country	Number of Passenger Cars	Population
Italy	31,953,247	57,816,000
Japan	42,655,000	127,635,000
Seychelles	6,970	80,000
United States	133,621,000	293,633,000
Democratic Republic of Congo	787,000	58,318,000

1. a. Which country has the most passenger cars?

b. Which country has the most passenger cars relative to its population? Explain.

When comparing ratios, such as the ones above, it is helpful to organize your data in a ratio table. You can round numbers in ratio tables, as shown below.

Italy

Number of Passenger Cars	32		
Popluation	58		

United States

Number of Passenger Cars	134		
Popluation	294		

2. a. Explain what is shown in the two ratio tables above.

b. How can you determine which country has more cars relative to its population, using the two ratio tables above?

Name ______________________ Date__________ Class__________

Car (page 2)

Country	Number of Passenger Cars	Population
Italy	31,953,247	57,816,000
Japan	42,655,000	127,635,000
Seychelles	6,970	80,000
United States	133,621,000	293,633,000
Democratic Republic of Congo	787,000	58,318,000

3. Order the five countries according to the number of cars relative to population.

____

____

____

____

____

4. You can express the relative number of cars in a country as the number of cars per 100 people. In Italy, for example, there are approximately 31.9 million passenger cars and 57.8 million people. This translates to 55 cars per 100 people.

a. Use a calculator to find the number of cars per 100 people for the five countries.

b. Explain why it is easier to compare "cars per 100 people" than "cars per person" or "cars per 10,000 people" in part **a** above.

Name ______________________ Date __________ Class __________

What Fractions?

The middle school in Woolton has 391 students. Fifty-one of the students are from a small town nearby, named Ridgeway. The principal claims, "One-eighth of our students are from Ridgeway."

1. Do you agree with the principal? Why or why not?

People sometimes round figures because precise amounts are not important in particular situations. Rounded figures are often better because they are easier to interpret and work with. Instead of saying "293 out of 391 students," for example, you can say "three-fourths of the students."

2. Use an easy-to-work-with fraction to describe each situation.

a. Six hundred fifteen readers have returned an opinion poll from *Radio Week* magazine. Three hundred ninety-seven say that WOLX is their favorite radio station.

b. Of those 615 respondents, 125 like listening to country music.

c. Fifty-nine of the 615 respondents regularly go to the movies.

d. The population of Albertville is 54,273,372. Of the people in Albertville, 9,012,461 are children under the age of 10.

e. In Dunhill, 9,321,989 people are under the age of 60. The population of Dunhill is 11,953,521.

f. The school library has 937 books, of which 240 are fiction.

g. There are 83 houses in Pilton, 63 of which are painted white.

h. Yesterday, Sondra counted her baseball cards and found that she had 78 of them. After giving some to a friend, she has 61 cards.

i. Juan had 52 baseball cards. After buying some more, he has a total of 75 cards.

Name ______________________ Date ____________ Class ____________

Watermelons (page 1)

Keith grows watermelons in his garden and then sells them for $1.80 per kilogram (kg). Watermelons usually do not weigh exactly one or two kilograms, so Keith uses a double number line to find the price of each one.

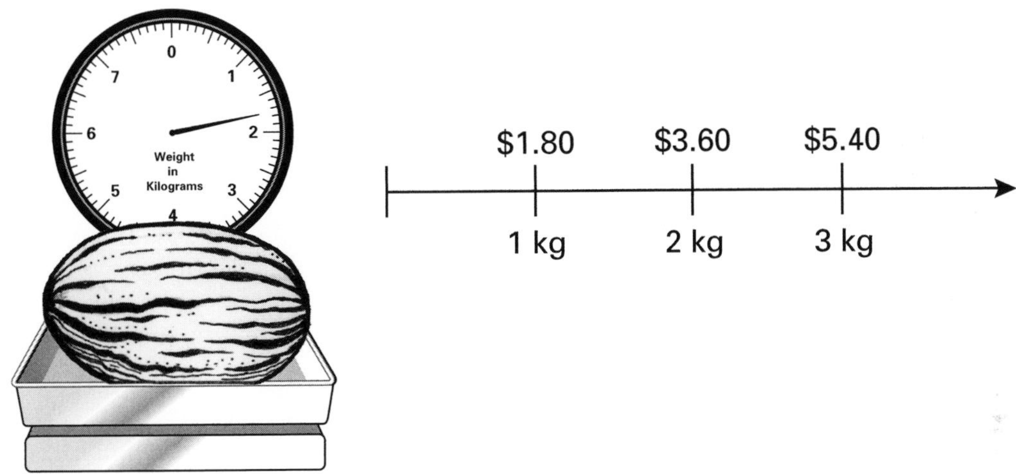

1. Explain how Keith finds the price of a watermelon weighing $1\frac{3}{4}$ kg by using the double number line.

2. Use a double number line to find the prices of watermelons that weigh the following amounts.

   a. $\frac{3}{4}$ kg

   b. $1\frac{1}{3}$ kg

   c. $2\frac{2}{3}$ kg

   d. $1\frac{1}{4}$ kg

   e. $1\frac{1}{2}$ kg

Name ______________________ Date ____________ Class ____________

Watermelons (page 2)

3. Keith lowers his price for watermelons to \$1.20 per kilogram. Revise the watermelon prices to reflect the sale price.

a. $\frac{3}{4}$ kg

b. $1\frac{1}{3}$ kg

c. $2\frac{2}{3}$ kg

d. $1\frac{1}{4}$ kg

e. $1\frac{1}{2}$ kg

If you have to calculate $\frac{1}{2} \times 1.20$, you can think of the problem: What will $\frac{1}{2}$ kg of watermelons cost, priced at \$1.20 per kilogram? Calculating $\frac{1}{2} \times 1.20$ is the same as calculating $\frac{1}{2}$ of 1.20.

4. Complete each of the following calculations. Show your work.

a. $1\frac{1}{3} \times 1.80$

b. $2\frac{3}{4} \times 1.60$

c. $1\frac{2}{3} \times 3.60$

d. $\frac{3}{4}$ of 0.80

e. $2\frac{1}{4}$ of 0.40

Name ______________________ Date____________ Class__________

Jim runs a produce stand at the market. Jim is too busy at the stand to use a calculator, so he has become very good at calculating prices mentally. To make calculations easier, he rounds the amounts shown on the scale to the nearest benchmark fraction.

1. If one kilogram of grapes costs $1.60, find the prices that Jim will charge for the following amounts of grapes.

a.

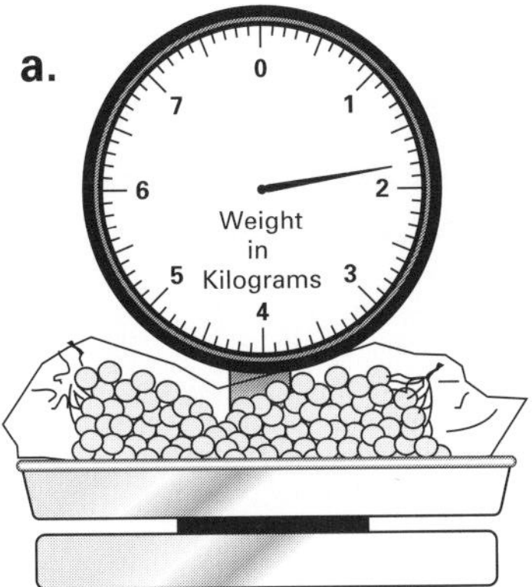

b.

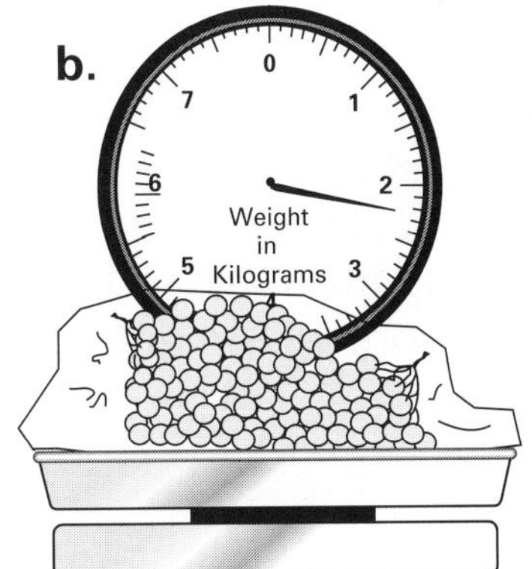

c.

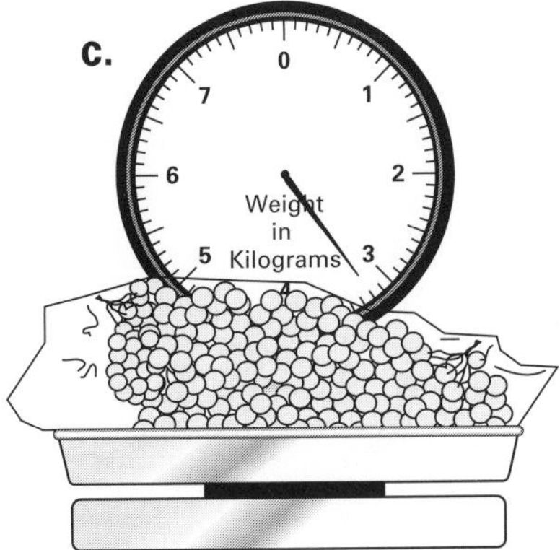

d.

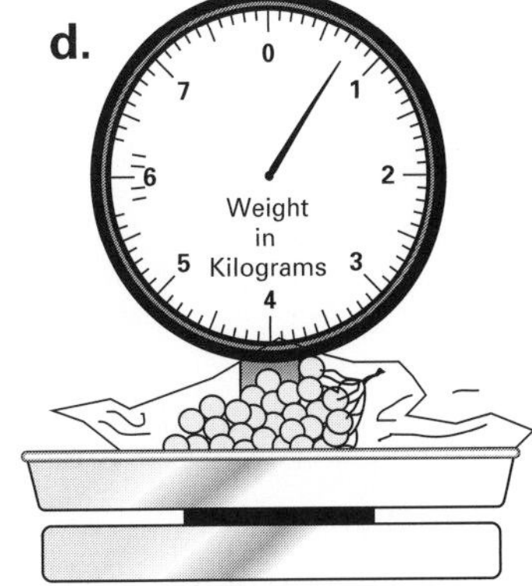

Name ______________________ Date__________ Class__________

At the Market (page 2)

2. One day Jim's scale breaks down, so he borrows a digital scale that shows the weight of items in very precise decimal notation. For the first four items that Jim sells, the scale indicates the following weights: 2.212, 0.760, 1.461, and 2.110. Explain why the decimal scale might be more difficult for Jim to use.

3. Jim decides to convert the weights shown on the decimal scale to the nearest benchmark fraction. For example, if the scale shows 1.739, Jim converts this decimal to $1\frac{3}{4}$. Convert each of the following decimals to fractions that will be easy for Jim to work with mentally.

a. 2.772 kg

b. 3.236 kg

c. 1.401 kg

d. 2.352 kg

e. 2.534 kg

f. 1.690 kg

g. 2.110 kg

h. 3.728 kg

i. 0.317 kg

j. 2.289 kg

Name ______________________ Date____________ Class____________

4. Find the price that Jim will charge for each of the following by first converting the decimal to a benchmark fraction and then using a mental calculation or a double number line strategy.

   a. 1.327 kg of white grapes at $2.10 per kilogram

   b. 3.532 kg of apples at $1.10 per kilogram

   c. 0.728 kg of oranges at $4.00 per kilogram

   d. 0.229 kg of potatoes at $0.80 per kilogram

   e. 3.996 kg of watermelon at $1.80 per kilogram

Name ______________________ Date__________ Class__________

Fraction of a Fraction

1. One-half of the students in Ms. Abel's class are girls, and $\frac{1}{3}$ of the girls have brown hair. If there are four girls in the class who have brown hair, how many students are there in Ms. Abel's class?

2. One-third of the students in Mr. Tolme's class are boys, and $\frac{1}{2}$ of the boys play a musical instrument. How many boys in Mr. Tolme's class play a musical instrument? Note that many answers are possible.

3. One-fourth of the students at Milton Middle School get a ride to school. One-half of these students ride with their parents. What fraction of the students ride with their parents?

4. Find the answer to each of the following.

a. $\frac{1}{2}$ of $\frac{1}{4}$ mile

b. $\frac{1}{3}$ of $\frac{1}{2}$ an hour

c. $\frac{1}{2}$ of $\frac{1}{3}$ an hour

d. $\frac{1}{3}$ of $\frac{1}{3}$ liter

e. $\frac{1}{2}$ of $\frac{1}{5}$ kilometer

f. $\frac{1}{4}$ of $\frac{1}{3}$ meter

g. $\frac{1}{3}$ of $\frac{3}{4}$ kilogram

h. $\frac{1}{2}$ of $\frac{2}{3}$ of the boys

i. $\frac{3}{4}$ of $\frac{1}{2}$ cup

j. $\frac{2}{3}$ of $\frac{2}{3}$ of the girls

Name ______________________ Date__________ Class__________

The Deli

Amy is buying some meat and cheese at the deli. Swiss cheese costs $3.60 per pound (lb), but Amy needs only 0.75 lb. She uses the following arrow string to compute how much 0.75 lb of Swiss cheese will cost.

$$\$3.60 \xrightarrow{\div 4} \$0.90 \xrightarrow{\times 3} \$2.70$$

1. Explain Amy's method.

2. Solve Amy's problem using a ratio table.

3. Find the prices for these purchases at the deli. Show how you found each price.

a. Ham costs $3.20 per pound. How much does 0.75 lb cost?

b. Cheddar cheese costs $7.50 per pound. How much does 0.80 lb cost?

c. Salami costs $4.00 per pound. How much does 0.40 lb cost?

d. Bologna costs $3.00 per pound. How much does 0.60 lb cost?

e. Pepperoni costs $2.40 per pound. How much does 1.25 lb cost?

f. Carol pays $1.80 for 0.75 lb of American cheese. What is the price per pound of American cheese?

Name ______________________ Date__________ Class__________

Percents (page 1)

To celebrate spring, Teri's Boutique is having its annual *Temperature Sale!*

The sale price depends on the current temperature outside. Today, the current temperature is 85°F, so the sale price of any item in the store is 85% of the regular price.

Anwar wants to buy a jacket, regularly priced at $140. What is the sale price?

Anwar uses a percent bar to begin his calculation.

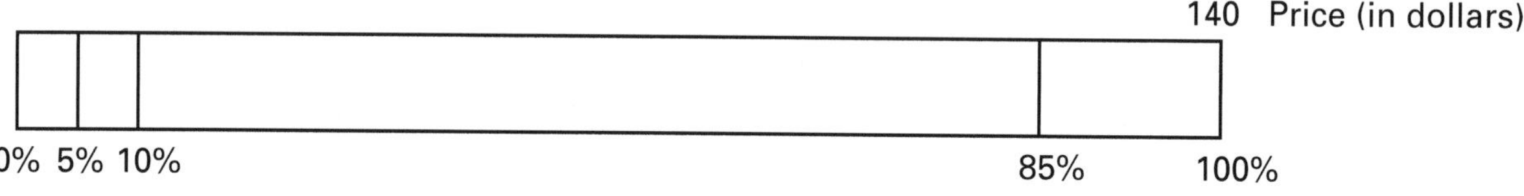

1. Finish Anwar's strategy to calculate the sale price of the jacket.

Sondra wants to buy a sweater, regularly priced at $55. What is the sale price?

Sondra uses a ratio table to begin her calculation.

Price (in dollars)	55	5.5			
Percentage	100	10			

2. Finish Sondra's strategy to calculate the sale price of the sweater.

3. Use a ratio table to find the sale price for each of the following.

Temperature Sale!			
	Regular Price	**Current Temperature**	**Sale Price**
a.	$24	75°F	
b.	$80	64°F	
c.	$90	72°F	

Name ______________________ Date ____________ Class ____________

Solve the following problems. Show your strategy.

On Wednesday, the temperature was 60°F .

4. a. Julius bought a pair of shoes for $48.
What was the original price?

b. Samantha bought a blouse for $12.
What was the original price?

Two weeks later, Tim bought a pair of shorts for $22. The original price was $55.

5. What was the temperature that day?

There are three main types of percentage problems.

i. Calculate the part.

ii. Calculate the total.

iii. Calculate the percent.

6. For the following percent bars, identify which type of problem (**i**, **ii**, or **iii**) is involved. Then calculate the missing numbers.

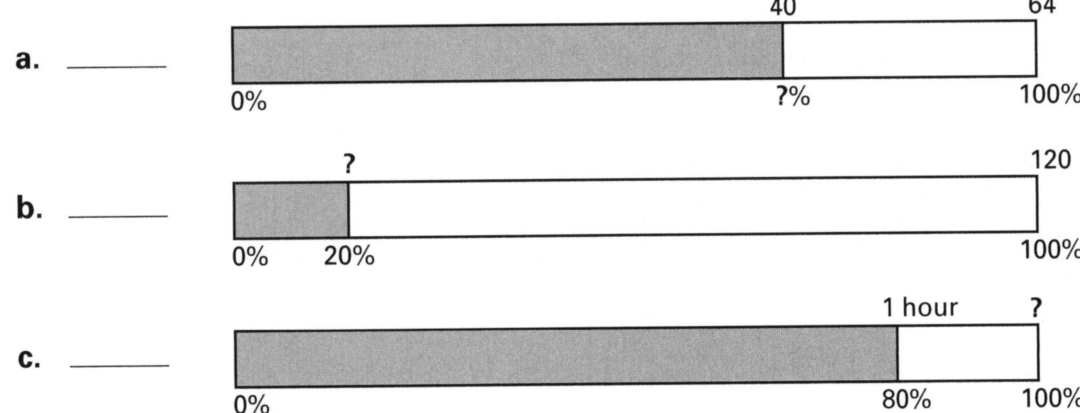

Name ______________________ Date ____________ Class ____________

Area Model (page 1)

Here is a scaled drawing of a beautiful square terrace. Each tile is imported from Italy and measures 1 m by 1 m.

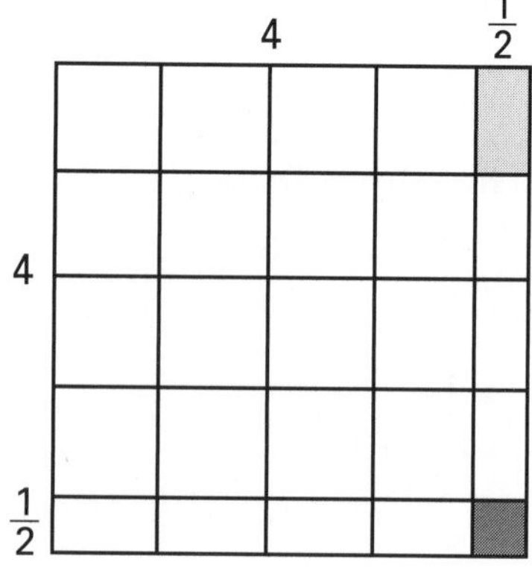

1. a. A small part of a tile is colored gray. What fractional part of a tile is this piece?

b. And the part in the bottom right corner?

c. Use this drawing to calculate the area of the whole terrace.

2. A smaller square terrace has side lengths of $3\frac{1}{2}$ m. Calculate the area of this terrace. Show your work.

3. a. On the drawing, label the area of each of the parts.

b. What is $(7\frac{1}{2})^2 = ?$

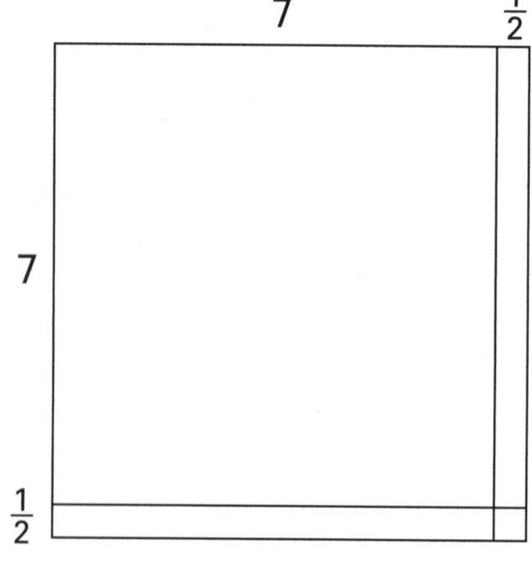

4. a. On the drawing, label the area of each of the parts.

b. What is $(6\frac{1}{3})^2 = ?$

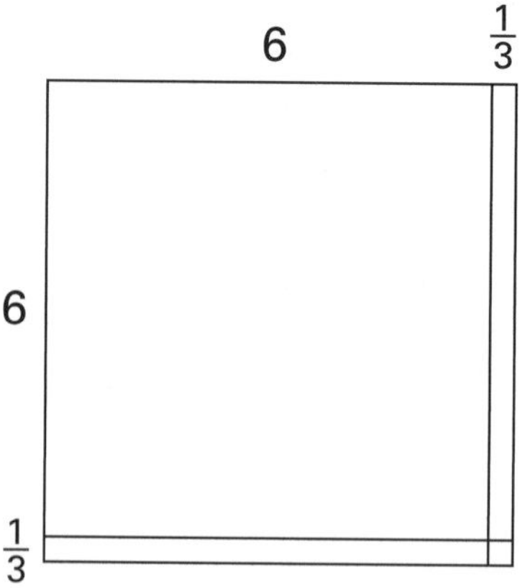

Name ______________________ Date______________ Class______________

Area Model (page 2)

5. Write the multiplication problem represented by this rectangle.

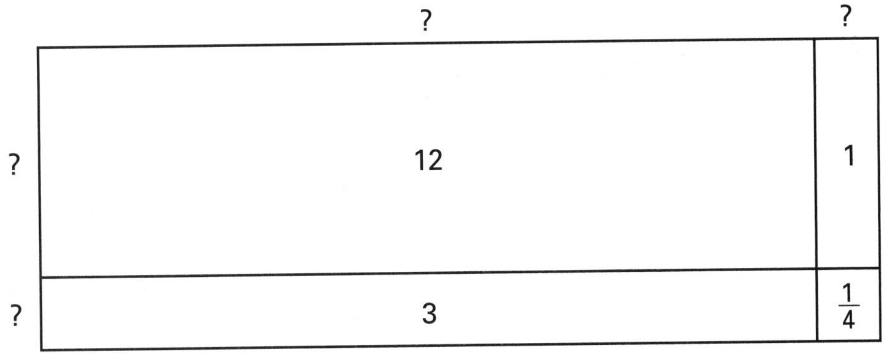

	?	?
?	12	1
?	3	$\frac{1}{4}$

6. Write the problem represented by this square.

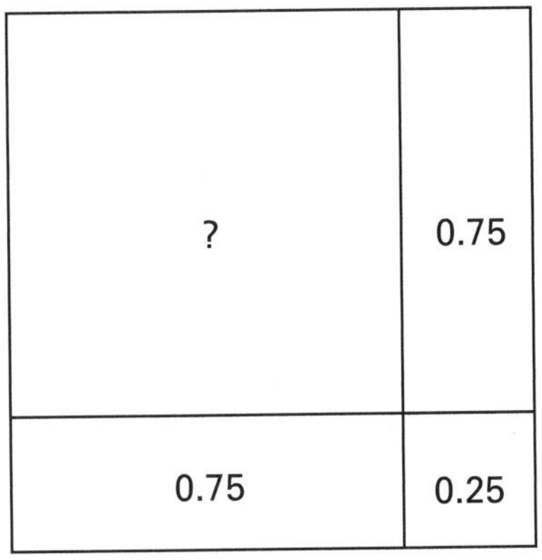

?	0.75
0.75	0.25

7. Make up your own area model problem. Ask a classmate to solve your problem.

Name ______________________ Date ______________ Class ______________

Scale (page 1)

To find the area of a space, it is important to write the dimension as a single unit, using either fractions or decimals.
For example, 7' 6" is $7\frac{1}{2}$' or 7.5'.

1. Write the dimensions of each room as a single unit.

a. Bedroom 10' 3" × 16' 6" ______________

b. Family Room 16' 9" × 15' 4" ______________

Here you see a drawing of the bedroom. Note that this drawing is not to scale.

2. Fill in the missing numbers and calculate the area of the bedroom in square feet.

A common scale for working with floor plans is 1":48". So one inch in the drawing is 48 inches in reality.

3. Use the scale line to find the actual dimensions of this bathroom using inches.

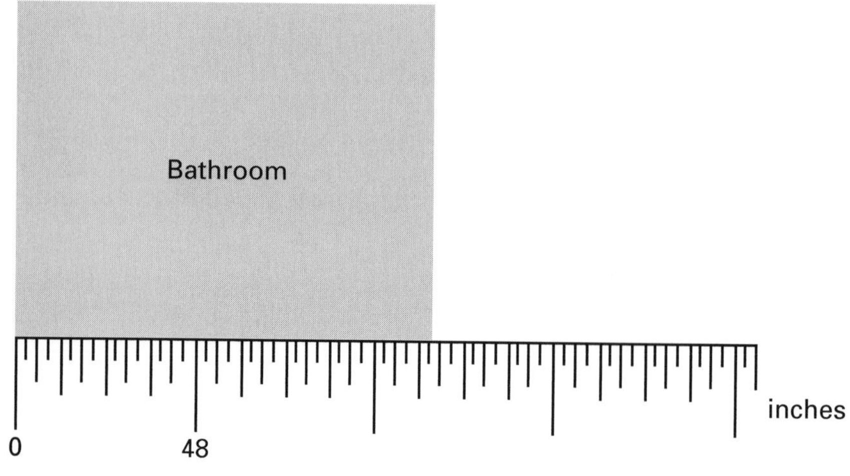

Scale (page 2)

The scale 1″:48″ is often written as 1″:4′, and called a *quarter-inch scale*.

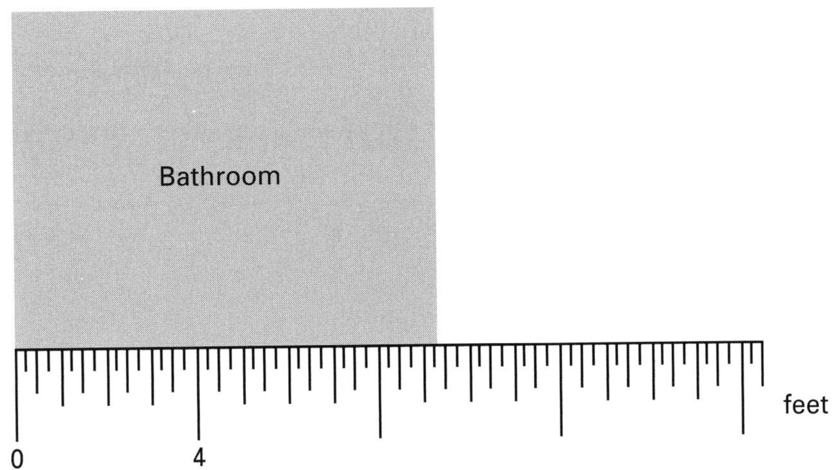

4. a. Use this scale line to find the actual dimensions of the bathroom using feet.

b. How can you use both scale lines to find the dimensions of the bathroom using a whole number of feet and inches?

5. Make a scale drawing of the two rooms in problem 1 on a quarter-inch scale.

Name ______________________ Date ____________ Class ____________

The Bus Company

A bus company requested two proposals for placing bus stops along a six-mile bus route.

Proposal I has stops every $\frac{3}{4}$ of a mile.

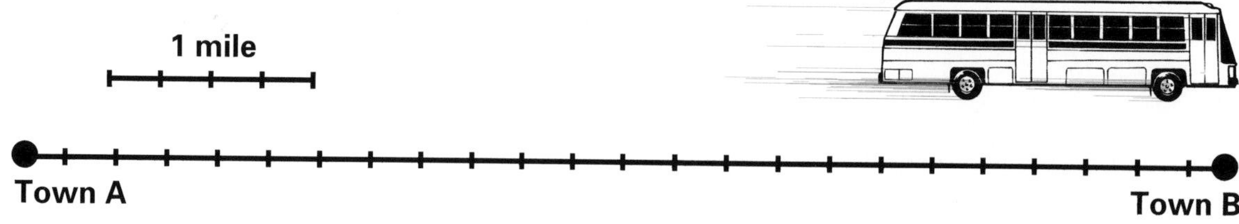

1. a. How many stops will there be?

   b. Use the scale line to help you accurately mark all of the proposed bus stops on the number line route above.

Proposal II has stops every $\frac{3}{8}$ of a mile.

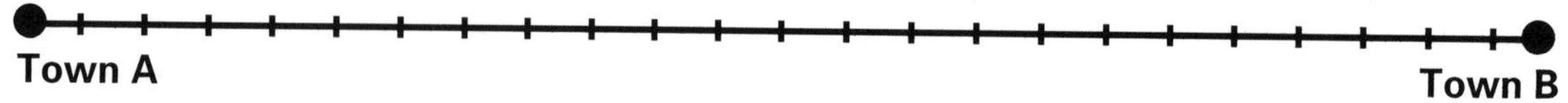

2. a. How many stops will there be?

   b. Use the scale line to help you accurately mark all of the proposed bus stops on the number line route above.

3. Show both proposals by filling in this ratio table. Start with the ones that are the easiest to calculate! Whenever possible, simplify your answers. Two answers have been done for you.

Stop Number	1	2	3	4	5	6	7	8	9	10
Proposal I Distance (in mi)	$\frac{3}{4}$	$1\frac{1}{2}$	$2\frac{1}{4}$							
Proposal II Distance (in mi)	$\frac{3}{8}$									

Name ______________________ Date ____________ Class ____________

During a marathon run, you have to drink enough water to stay hydrated. Volunteers along the race course hand out plastic cups of water. One cup holds about $\frac{1}{8}$ liter.

1. Susan's trainer suggests that she drink a total of $2\frac{1}{2}$ liters during the race. How many cups should she grab throughout the race? Show your work.

For allergies, Noelle's doctor prescribed $\frac{1}{4}$ of a tablet, three times a day. Today, there are 12 tablets left until she needs a refill.

2. How many days will these 12 tablets last her? Show your work.

Here is the way Mark calculates $1\frac{3}{4} \div \frac{1}{8}$.

$1\frac{3}{4} \div \frac{1}{8} =$

$\frac{7}{4} \div \frac{1}{8} =$

$\frac{14}{8} \div \frac{1}{8} = 14$

Mark

3. Explain Mark's strategy.

4. Use Mark's strategy to calculate:

   a. $3\frac{1}{3} \div \frac{1}{6}$ b. $2\frac{1}{7} \div \frac{1}{14}$

Mark uses the same strategy to divide by a mixed number. For example, $4\frac{3}{4} \div 1\frac{1}{8}$.

$4\frac{3}{4} \div 1\frac{1}{8} =$

$\frac{19}{4} \div \frac{9}{8} =$

$\frac{38}{8} \div \frac{9}{8} =$

$38 \div 9 = 4\frac{2}{9}$

Mark

5. Use Mark's strategy to calculate:

   a. $5\frac{1}{6} \div 1\frac{1}{3}$ b. $3\frac{1}{10} \div 2\frac{1}{5}$

Name ________________________ Date ____________ Class ____________

With and Without a Calculator

1. Use your calculator to find the cost of the following items. Note that stores round up all prices to the nearest cent.

   a. 1.365 kilograms of pears at $3.10 per kilogram

   b. 0.723 kg of broccoli at $3.25 per kilogram

   c. 1.739 kg of collard greens at $1.79 per kilogram

   d. 1.396 kg of strawberries at $1.65 per kilogram

   e. 0.842 kg of oranges at $2.98 per kilogram

Michelle is supposed to use her calculator to do her homework, but the decimal point key is broken. To calculate the price of 1.293 kg of spinach that costs $2.98 per kilogram, Michelle enters 1293 × 298, and her calculator displays 385314. She can then figure out where to place the decimal point by estimating the correct answer.

2. Without using your calculator, find the answer to 1.293 × $2.98. Explain your strategy.

3. Without using your calculator, help Michelle find the correct price for each of the following items.

   a. 3.129 kg of grapes, selling for $3.10 per kilogram (Michelle's calculator displays 969990.)

   b. 21.38 kg of apples, selling for $1.26 per kilogram (Michelle's calculator displays 269388)

   c. 0.729 kg of lemons, selling for $4.10 per kilogram (Michelle's calculator displays 298890.)

   d. 3.28 kg of oranges, selling for $4.98 per kilogram (Michelle's calculator displays 163344.)

   e. 0.083 kg of parsley, selling for $5.50 per kilogram (Michelle's calculator displays 45650).

Name ______________________ Date ____________ Class ____________

Estimations

Animations

To make an animation, you need many pictures to show movement. Hand-drawn animations need 12 frames per second.

1. Estimate how many pictures you will need to draw for a 5-minute cartoon.

Leaking Faucet

Each second, two drops drip from this leaking faucet.

It takes 20 drops to fill one cubic centimeter. Recall that 1 liter fits exactly into one cubic decimeter. Pete's father puts a 10-liter bucket under the tap to catch the water.

2. Will this bucket be large enough to catch all the water during the night, from 8 P.M. till 8 A.M.? Justify your opinion.

New York Marathon

About 30,000 runners sign up to run in the annual New York Marathon.

3. Estimate how long the line of 30,000 participating runners might be. Show your assumptions.

4. A reporter at the race stated that more than two million spectators stood along the route. Does this number make sense? Show your reasoning.

Name ____________________ Date __________ Class __________

Serial Numbers

The Green Air factory makes refrigerators.

A serial number is etched into each refrigerator in sequential order. Here are the serial numbers of the first three refrigerators made last Tuesday.

SR–341–05–0193

SR–341–05–0194

SR–341–05–0195

1. List the last four digits of the serial numbers of the next three refrigerators made at the Green Air factory.

Here are the serial numbers of the last three refrigerators made last Tuesday.

SR–341–05–3601

SR–341–05–3602

SR–341–05–3603

2. How many refrigerators were made last Tuesday?

Last Wednesday, the serial number SR–341–05–3604 was etched into the first refrigerator made, and the last refrigerator made had the serial number SR–341–05–7702.

3. How many refrigerators were made last Wednesday?

The last refrigerator made on Thursday had the serial number SR–341–05–9871, and the last refrigerator made on Friday had the serial number SR–341–06–3004.

4. How many refrigerators were made on Thursday? And on Friday?

Name ______________________ Date ______________ Class ______________

Bar Code (page 1)

Almost all products sold today have a bar code. For retail items, the bar code has a length of 13 digits. It shows information about the county of origin, the manufacturer, and the product. The last digit is a safeguard to check the other twelve digits.

112233445566?

This barcode has only twelve digits; it is missing the safeguard digit.

1. Carry out these calculations to find the missing last digit.

   Step 1 Starting from the left, add all digits in the odd position.

   Step 2 Multiply the result by 3.

   Step 3 Add all digits in the even position.

   Step 4 Add the results of Step 2 and Step 3.

   Step 5 Determine what number needs to be added to the result of Step 4 to make it divisible by 10.

Here is a different barcode.

2. Verify that this bar code has a correct safeguard digit.

Here is a copy of the barcode for a new book.

3. Find the correct safeguard digit for this book.

Name ______________________ Date__________ Class__________

Bar Code (page 2)

There is also an ISBN number located across the top of the barcode. This number contains information about the country, the publisher, and the title of the book. The last digit is the safeguard digit.

The safeguard digit for an ISBN code is calculated differently from the safeguard digit of the barcode below it.

4. Use the following steps to find the safeguard digit of the ISBN number 90–270–1165-?

Step 1: Multiply the first digit by 10,
the second digit by 9,
the third digit by 8,
and so on. Then add the results.

Step 2: Determine what number you
have to add to the result in Step 1
to make it evenly divisible by 11.

5. Verify that this book, *Number Tools*, has a correct safeguard digit for the ISBN number.

Here is some additional information you might find interesting.

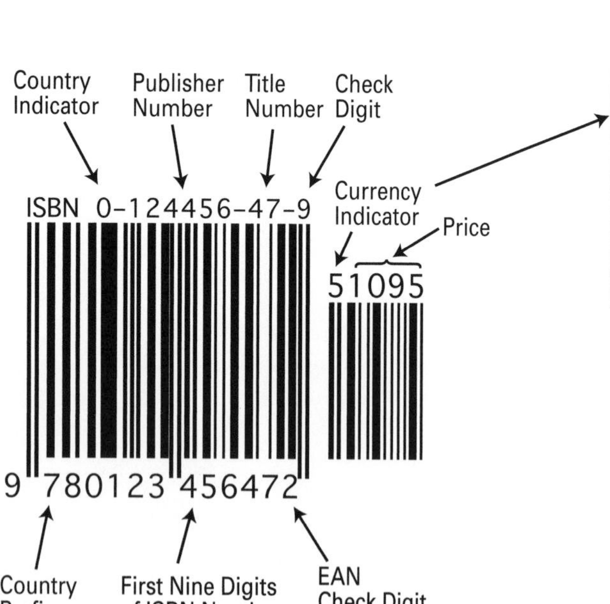

First digit "5" for U.S. dollars
First digit "6" for Canadian dollars
First digit "4" for New Zealand dollars
First digit "3" for Australian dollars
First digit "0" and "1" for British pounds
59999 is used for price of $100 or more ($U.S.)
90000 means "Price is not included."

6. Look for another book and use this information to decode its barcode.